Livy *History of Rome* I

The following titles are available from Bloomsbury for the OCR specifications in Latin and Greek for examinations from June 2021 to June 2023

Catullus: A Selection of Poems, with introduction, commentary notes and vocabulary by John Godwin

Cicero *Pro Cluentio*: A Selection, with introduction, commentary notes and vocabulary by Matthew Barr

Livy *History of Rome* I: A Selection, with introduction, commentary notes and vocabulary by John Storey

Ovid *Heroides*: A Selection, with introduction, commentary notes and vocabulary by Christina Tsaknaki

Tacitus *Annals* IV: A Selection, with introduction, commentary notes and vocabulary by Robert Cromarty

Virgil *Aeneid* XII: A Selection, with introduction, commentary notes and vocabulary by James Burbidge

OCR Anthology for Classical Greek AS and A Level, covering the prescribed texts by Aristophanes, Homer, Plato, Plutarch, Sophocles and Thucydides, with introduction, commentary notes and vocabulary by Simon Allcock, Sam Baddeley, John Claughton, Alastair Harden, Sarah Harden, Carl Hope and Jo Lashley

Supplementary resources for these volumes can be found at www.bloomsbury.com/OCR-editions-2021-2023 Please type the URL into your web browser and follow the instructions to access the Companion Website. If you experience any problems, please contact Bloomsbury at academicwebsite@bloomsbury.com

Livy *History of Rome* I: A Selection

Chapters 53–54, 56 (*haec agenti* . . .)–60

With introduction, commentary notes and vocabulary by John Storey

BLOOMSBURY ACADEMIC
LONDON • NEW YORK • OXFORD • NEW DELHI • SYDNEY

BLOOMSBURY ACADEMIC
Bloomsbury Publishing Plc
50 Bedford Square, London, WC1B 3DP, UK
1385 Broadway, New York, NY 10018, USA

BLOOMSBURY, BLOOMSBURY ACADEMIC and the Diana logo are
trademarks of Bloomsbury Publishing Plc

First published in Great Britain 2020

Cover design: Terry Woodley
Cover image © PjrTravel / Alamy Stock Photo

A catalogue record for this book is available from the British Library.

A catalog record for this book is available from the Library of Congress.

ISBN: PB: 978-1-3500-6038-8
         ePDF: 978-1-3500-6040-1
         eBook: 978-1-3500-6039-5

Typeset by RefineCatch Limited, Bungay, Suffolk

To find out more about our authors and books visit
www.bloomsbury.com and sign up for our newsletters.

Contents

Preface

The text and notes found in this volume are designed to guide any student who has mastered Latin up to GCSE level and wishes to read a selection of Livy's *History of Rome* in the original.

The edition is, however, particularly designed to support students who are reading Livy's text in preparation for OCR's A-Level Latin examination in June 2022–June 2023.

Livy's monumental *History of Rome*, originally totalling 142 books, covered the period from the city's legendary foundation by Romulus to his own day – the Principate of Augustus. Book I, from which the present selection is taken, covered the reigns of the seven kings of Rome concluding with that of Tarquinius Superbus and the foundation of Republican government that followed.

This edition contains a detailed introduction to the context of Livy's *History*, supported by a family tree covering the last kings of Rome. The notes to the text itself aim to help students bridge the gap between GCSE and A-Level Latin, and focus therefore on the harder points of grammar and word order. At the end of the book is a full vocabulary list for all the words contained in the prescribed sections, with words in OCR's Defined Vocabulary List for AS Level Latin flagged by means of an asterisk.

I am grateful to Alice Wright and Helen Tredget at Bloomsbury for their guidance and support in the production of this edition, and to the two anonymous reviewers who offered immeasurably useful feedback on both the Introduction and the Commentary; needless to say, such errors as remain are my own.

John Storey
March 2019

Introduction

Livy

Little is known of the life of Titus Livius whom we call Livy – even his dates of birth and death have been debated, although it is generally now believed that he lived from 59 BC to AD 17. He was born in Patavium (modern Padua), a town in Northern Italy which at that time belonged to the Province of Cisalpine Gaul, and it is possible that he returned there before his death, having spent most of his life in Rome.

Livy's education seems primarily to have been in Patavium: unlike contemporary well-to-do young men, such as Horace, he was not sent by his parents to Athens, and there is evidence in his work both of a limited fluency in Greek, and a lack of geographical precision which may suggest that he was not widely travelled. Another contemporary, Asinius Pollio, is said to have criticized Livy's writing for its *Patavinitas* – his 'Patavianness' which might imply a certain 'provinciality' – although whether this comment is primarily on his style or his politics is unclear: Patavium was a staunchly Republican, liberty-loving, city, while Pollio had sided with Caesar in the Civil War of 49–45 BC. It is equally unclear whether Livy's apparently restricted education was consequent on the turbulent politics of exactly that period when he might otherwise have been sent away, or on his family circumstances. Of the latter we know nothing.

Although a reference by Livy to *Caesar Augustus* (I.19.3) must postdate 27 BC when Octavian assumed the name Augustus, the traditional view that he wrote his history from that date onwards has more recently come under review. The consensus now is that Book I, as we have it, is a second edition, and that Livy began writing in the mid-30s BC by which time he was living in Rome. There is no record of his having been actively engaged in politics or the law-courts, nor evidence of literary patronage as enjoyed, for example, by Virgil or Horace. Livy's reputation – he had written a couple of minor philosophical dialogues which sadly have not survived – gained him an acquaintance with Augustus himself, but they were not close. The Princeps is said to have disapproved of his treatment of recent history, and it seems that those books dealing with Augustus' own reign were not published until after his death in AD 14. We must presume, therefore, that Livy came to Rome to access records that would enable him to write the magnum opus that he had conceived – a history of Rome from its foundation to the present – and that he was able to support himself in this enterprise.

Ab Urbe Condita

It is by this title, 'From the Foundation of the City', that Livy's History is generally known. He dedicated his whole life to its composition, writing in total 142 books. Of these, regrettably, only 35 are extant, but for almost all others there exist summaries of varying length that enable us to appreciate the scope of the work. After a Preface on the task of writing history, Livy begins with the establishment of a settlement by the Trojan exile Aeneas, moving swiftly on to the birth and life of Romulus and Remus, and the foundation of Rome, traditionally dated to 753 BC. Book I – from which the present selection is taken – treats the Regal Period when Rome was ruled by a succession of seven kings, and the establishment of the Republic by Brutus in 510/509 BC.

Livy and the Age of Augustus

It is a given of historiography, ancient and modern, that no author can remain uninfluenced by the events of his own era, however detached or unbiased he might attempt to be. Livy lived through a period of significant political change and upheaval: the Republic eventually gave way to the Principate of Augustus, but only after a series of divisive and bloody civil wars. Livy's History was written almost entirely under the Augustan Principate, a period that no one would have dared to describe as monarchic, and yet one which bore all the hallmarks of monarchy.

It is only possible here to give a very brief account of the period, and the student is recommended to read more widely in order to gain a greater understanding and appreciation of the context in which Livy was writing. Particular attention is drawn to those events which have a direct bearing on how Livy wrote about, and how we might read, the episodes included in the present selection.

The Late Republican period had been dominated by the political influence of powerful individuals, backed up by armies that increasingly owed a loyalty to them rather than to the state. The institutions of government – of which the Republicans in the Senate remained so proud – had gradually been subverted by the reforming agenda of the Gracchi, the Marian reforms of the army, and Sulla's dictatorship. In 59 BC the three most dominant men of the age, Julius Caesar, Crassus and Pompey, came together in an unofficial strategic alliance later termed 'The First Triumvirate'.

Following the death of Crassus in 53 BC, the Triumvirate seemed to have outlived its viability: Pompey, with Senatorial support, found himself directly opposed to Caesar's interests, and after a political stand-off the latter marched the army with which he had been conquering Gaul across the River Rubicon in January 49 BC. It was not lawful for a Roman general to lead his army into Italy in this fashion, and Pompey responded by leaving for Greece from where he would oppose Caesar. So began an intense and brutal civil war which lasted from 49–45 BC. Caesar was ultimately victorious, and became de facto ruler of Rome as dictator. The dictatorship was not un-Republican – it had been created to allow an individual to take complete control of affairs in an emergency, but as such was normally limited by time to six months, or the emergency, whichever was shorter.

On the Ides of March 44 BC Julius Caesar was assassinated. The conspirators were Republicans fearing that Caesar – who now had himself declared Dictator Perpetuus, or Dictator for Life – was trying to re-establish a monarchy. Monarchy was anathema to the Roman political community: the kings, of whom Livy writes in Book I, had ultimately proven themselves corrupt and unjust. The overthrow of the last king, Tarquinius Superbus, by Lucius Junius Brutus (Chapters 59–60) was celebrated as the foundation of the Republic, with Brutus himself becoming one of the first consuls. Among the conspirators was Caesar's friend Marcus Junius Brutus, a man who claimed direct descent from that Brutus who established the Republic, and who undoubtedly believed that in killing Caesar he was saving it. If the conspirators believed that the death of Caesar would result in the restoration of traditional government they were sadly mistaken. Instead there followed a renewed period of bloody civil strife.

Into the chaotic political maelstrom of the Late Republic had been born Livy; so too his almost exact contemporary Gaius Octavius Thurinus, born 23 September 63 BC. Octavius was, on his mother's side, a great-nephew of Julius Caesar who, it seems, lacking a legitimate son himself, took great interest in the boy and supported his early political and military career. In his will Caesar adopted Octavius as son and heir – from that date we refer to him as Octavian. The Republican faction courted the young, and now militarily powerful, Octavian, but ultimately his determination to avenge his great-uncle, and shrewd political calculation, led him to side with Marcus Antonius in a new civil war against the conspirators. This war ended with the two Battles of Philippi in October 42 BC. By then a formal, and legal, political alliance had been agreed between Octavian, Marcus Antonius, and another influential Caesarian, Marcus Aemilius Lepidus: the Second Triumvirate.

The Second Triumvirate held an uneasy peace between Octavian and Marcus Antonius for nearly ten years – they divided both the government and empire between them in a series of agreements. Lepidus was removed from the Triumvirate in the aftermath of a war on Sicily against Sextus Pompeius in 36 BC: the troubles caused by the breakdown of functional Republican government had not ended at Philippi. By the late 30s BC the remaining Triumvirs were at loggerheads, and by 31 BC they were at war. Marcus Antonius, supported by his lover Cleopatra the Queen of Egypt, was defeated by Octavian's forces in the naval Battle of Actium in September 31 BC. They were pursued back to Egypt where they both committed suicide. Both before and in the aftermath of this campaign, Octavian and his propagandists made much of Antonius' royal pretentions which had threatened to tear the Roman Republic apart. Octavian was determined to present himself as the restorer of the Republic, although he had no intention of truly surrendering the power that he had acquired over the preceding decade.

This posed a difficult challenge for Octavian: how could he maintain one-man rule without being perceived to be a monarch. He was determined not to make the same mistake as Caesar. Initially, he opted to continue to hold one of the two Consulships – that supreme, annually elected and collegiate office of Republican government. By 27 BC, with the crisis clearly over, the unconstitutional nature of his position worried him enough that he placed the matter before the Senate. They confirmed him in his annual Consulships, and heaped further honours upon him, including the name *Augustus* by which he was known from then onwards, and the title *Princeps*. Again in 23 BC, Augustus became sufficiently concerned about how his status was understood that he resigned the Consulship, releasing it back to Senatorial election. In response, however, the Senate now granted him a series of new powers that confirmed him as leader of the state with greater authority than any elected magistrate both in Rome and in the provinces. It was the powers granted in 23 BC that formed the basis of Imperial, monarchic, rule for centuries to come – couched in legal, republican terms.

Augustus ruled Rome from his victory at Actium in 31 BC until his death on 19 August 14 AD. He wished to present this as a new golden age of Roman peace and prosperity – as represented on the monumental Ara Pacis commissioned by the Senate in 13 BC, and completed in 9 BC. Augustus regarded the collapse of the old Republic as having been in large part caused by the social and moral debasement of the age. He was determined to solve this. He introduced sumptuary laws, restricting public and private extravagance, and most notably legislated to curb sexual immorality in the Leges Juliae of 18–17 BC. These, of course, postdate the composition of Book I of Livy's work, but Augustus' preoccupation with the issue seems to have been a long-standing one, and, for good or ill, it had an impact on the output of several authors of the period. Livy's account of the rape of Lucretia, and its aftermath, may reflect something of the zeitgeist.

It was in this context that Livy began his History of Rome which he would frame chronologically. His first challenge, therefore, was how to write about a period of one-man rule brought to an end by a hero named Brutus without falling foul of the new regime at Rome.

Book I

In subsequent Books Livy would assume an annalistic framework in which events are recorded year by year and with some regularity of formula. This was impossible for the Regal Period – the records that would support his later work were lacking, and in any case the traditional dates for the reigns of the kings were largely speculative.

His sources for the period were earlier writers, and Livy's use of them was more creative than might be expected of a modern historian. On this point it should be observed that Livy was not a modern historian. If we were to criticize him for using sources with little discrimination, for failing to make clear what was fact and what interpretation, for allowing patriotism to colour his history, we would be failing to understand his writing. As a historian of the late first century BC his objectives were very different: to show how the greatness of Rome had been achieved by the wisdom and leadership of his ancestors, the firmness of the national character, and the support of the gods; to provide entertaining lessons in exemplary moral behaviour through stories of heroes of the Republican age. Judged on this basis, Livy is a highly successful historian. The Preface to Book I provides an interesting insight into Livy's aims and understanding of his task.

Book I opens with the arrival of Trojan exiles in Italy led by Aeneas who founds a settlement at Lavinium. This foundation myth is central to Virgil's epic poem the *Aeneid* which was written between 29–19 BC. It is likely that Livy and Virgil were known to one another at Rome, but there is no need to presume any interdependence: they were both working with a well-established narrative tradition. Aeneas's son Ascanius left Lavinium to found Alba Longa, and it was at Alba Longa that Romulus and Remus were born.

Chapters 4–16 deal with the birth of Romulus and Remus and the foundation of Rome in 753 BC. With Remus' death – notably at his brother's hands, foreshadowing future civil strife – Romulus became the first king of Rome. Livy's account of his reign focuses on his attempts to grow the population and influence of the city, not wholly by fair means as seen in the Rape of the Sabine women. Romulus did not die, but was rather bodily assumed into heaven to become a god (an alternative explanation being that he was ripped apart by senators when fog descended during a military review). There followed an interregnum of one year because there was no clear heir to Romulus' position.

Chapters 17–21: Numa Pompilius (715–673 BC) is credited with the organization of Roman state religion, and his reign was one of peace and stability. Many of the religious practices described remained current in Livy's time – in this sense Numa's rule provides an historical explanation for the existence of those priesthoods and rituals. Scholars tend to regard Romulus and Remus as mythological figures while Numa is considered to have been a more genuine historical figure.

Chapters 22–31 cover the reign of Tullus Hostilus (673–642 BC) whom Livy describes as being 'more warlike than Romulus had been'. Conflict with Alba Longa seemed inevitable – one city must give way to allow the other's influence to grow and flourish. The matter was initially settled by a combat between the three Horatii, fighting for Rome and the three Curatii, fighting for Alba Longa, it being considered that a protracted war would leave even the victor vulnerable to attack by the Etruscans. With two of his brothers dead, the remaining Horatius won, and so thereby did Rome. But the agreed-on alliance that followed was treacherously broken by the Alban king Mettius Fufetius who deserted Tullus in battle: he paid for his treachery with his life. Tullus settled the issue of territorial domination for good by having Alba Longa destroyed and its population moved to Rome. A further war against the Sabines allowed Tullus to further expand the sphere of Rome's control. Shortly thereafter Tullus died when his house was struck by a thunderbolt and consumed by flames.

Chapters 32–34: Ancus Marcius (642–617 BC) was next elected king at Rome, a grandson of Numa Pompilius. He was respectful of his grandfather's policy of piety and peace, but forced by circumstances to fight a war with the Latins; he accordingly instituted the rites of the Fetials by which war was formally and solemnly declared – it is notable that these rites were revived by Augustus as part of his restoration of religious tradition, who attended to them in 32 BC before the war with Antonius and Cleopatra. Under Ancus, Roman territory was further expanded south to the sea at the mouth of the River Tiber.

Chapters 35–40 record the reign of Tarquinius Priscus, the fifth king (616–579 BC), who succeeded after Ancus died of natural causes. The name Tarquinius is Etruscan: Rome was a melting-pot of Italian identities at this stage in its development as a city-state. Priscus was elected king over Ancus' own sons, there being no established tradition of hereditary monarchy. One of his first acts, Livy tells us, was to increase the roll of the Senate by a hundred. Among the clans included were the Octavii from whom Augustus was descended, although it is interesting that Livy does not draw attention to this point. Tarquinius waged a series of wars against Latin and Etruscan cities, considerably enriching Rome with the plunder and expanding the nascent empire. A number of building projects were commenced, paid for by the spoils, although there is a possibility that the reigns of the two Tarquinii have been conflated on this point. Tarquinius' choice of Servius Tullius – perhaps the son of a slave-woman – as son-in-law and heir provoked Ancus' sons, resentful at having been excluded from the kingship, to plot against him. The assassination attempt was successful, but Tanaquil, Tarquinius' wife, suppressed news of it until Servius Tullius' succession had been smoothly arranged. The sons of Ancus went into voluntary exile at Suessa Pometia – the town that Tarquinius Superbus would conquer so efficiently (Chapter 53).

Chapters 41–48 account for the sixth king, Servius Tullius' reign (578–535 BC). He cemented his rule by wars against Veii and the Etruscans; the *Fasti Triumphales* – a formal record of military successes probably engraved on the Arch of Augustus in 18 BC – show that he celebrated three triumphs. His domestic reforms included the extension of the franchise to lower orders within Roman society, the expansion of the city of Rome, and the construction of further temples. Servius had two daughters, both called Tullia. Thinking it a prudent, conciliatory and stabilizing move he married them to the two sons – or perhaps grandsons – of his predecessor,

Lucius and Arruns Tarquinius. An affair between Lucius Tarquinius and his brother's wife led quickly to their elimination of their siblings, and swift remarriage to each other. Already we start to get some impression of the character of Lucius Tarquinius Superbus, the final king of Rome. Livy sees the hand of Tullia firmly behind the murder of her sister and first husband, and then inspiring her second husband to rebel against her father. In this, we see echoes of contemporary presentations of Cleopatra as the power behind the madness of Marcus Antonius' actions against Octavian, as well as a Roman preoccupation with the dangers of powerful women. Tarquinius physically hurled Servius from the Senate House, sending men in pursuit to kill him. Tullia, we are told, was so inhuman that she had her chariot driven over the body of Servius – her own father. Livy is clear that her wicked deeds would haunt her, and returns to them in Chapter 59, when Tarquinius is overthrown in turn.

A family tree

It is useful at this stage to visualize the relationships between the main players in the selection that follows.

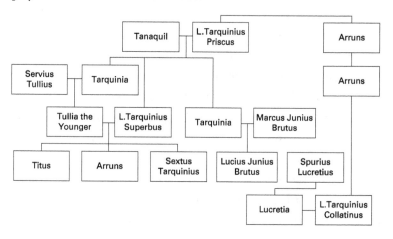

It will be clear from this diagram in particular how closely related Sextus Tarquinius, Lucius Junius Brutus and Lucretia in fact were.

The reign of Tarquinius Superbus

Livy begins his account of Tarquinius' reign with the comment, 'his conduct won him the cognomen of Superbus' – the Arrogant or the Proud. He immediately thereafter sets about detailing some of his most grievous acts. He denied burial to Servius Tullius, his predecessor and father-in-law, allegedly because Romulus too had had none. He had a number of senators who had favoured Servius killed, and, fearing the regicidal precedent he had set surrounded himself with a bodyguard. He granted himself complete power in the most serious of lawsuits, able then to impose death, exile or the forfeiture of property largely at will; this power he used against those he suspected, those he disliked and those whose goods he coveted – however innocent they might be. Unlike his predecessors he made policy decisions entirely without reference to the Senate, exercising a despotic authority: under Tarquinius Superbus the monarchy truly became the feared and loathed institution that it would remain throughout Roman Republican history.

Conscious of the risks to his position at Rome, Tarquinius wooed the Latins so that he might have allies close at hand, marrying his daughter to a prominent nobleman. Whether by design or accident, the events surrounding an assembly of the Latins allowed him to eliminate a prominent opponent, Turnus Herdonius. Tarquinius had summoned the Latin nobles to assemble on an important issue, but was then late in arriving; in his absence Turnus spoke vehemently against him. The king was annoyed by this and contrived to have a large quantity of swords hidden in Turnus' house. He then reported his fears that Turnus was plotting against him to the other Latin noblemen who, when they searched the house, found the evidence Tarquinius had predicted. Such was the resentment at this treachery that there was no trial: Turnus was drowned, apparently by his peers.

Praising their swift and decisive actions, Tarquinius seized the opportunity to renegotiate the relationship between the Romans and the Latins – undoubtedly to the advantage of the former. The Latins agreed, not least because they had just been given a clear example of how the king dealt with those who disagreed. Part of the treaty required that the Latins supply soldiers to a combined army – these were put under the command of Roman officers, and it was this army that enabled Tarquinius to pursue his military objectives, which Livy goes on to detail.

Such were Tarquinius Superbus' domestic policies that they enabled Livy to describe him at the start of Chapter 53 – where the present selection begins – as 'a king so unjust in peace'.

Livy's style

Just as Livy himself lived and wrote in that transitional period between Republic and Empire, so his style can be said to fall between that of the great prose authors of the previous generation – chiefly Cicero – and those of the latter first century AD – among them Seneca and Tacitus.

Like his predecessors, Livy has a tendency to employ long, elaborately constructed sentences: subordinate clauses abound, and identifying the main verb is often essential in trying to gain an understanding of the structure as a whole. Livy wrote to be read rather than to be heard, and in consequence his sentences can, at times, be even more elaborate than those of Cicero. However, **variatio** also plays a part in Livy's style: a history that comprised only long sentences would quickly become boring. He tends to deploy longer structures while explaining the circumstances, switching to shorter sentences as events take over. This is illustrated, for example, in 56.4–6: long sentences establish the reasons for the embassy to Delphi, but the departure of the principal ambassadors is given in a very brief one: 'Titus et Arruns profecti.'

The omission of 'sunt' in the example just given is one of a number of means by which Livy creates a dramatic and lively pace within his narrative. The **Historic Present** – for example 58.11 'in corde defigit', as Lucretia takes her own life – gives a vivid immediacy, drawing the reader into the action, and is a common feature of Livy's prose. So too is the **Historic Infinitive**, found, for example, in 54.1 to show the speed with which Sextus is able to take control of affairs in Gabii. The combination of this with **asyndeton** at 58.3 conveys something of the breathless urgency with which he later attempts to seduce Lucretia.

It will be noted that aspects of Livy's use of language are distinctly poetic, and he does not hesitate to use graphic descriptions – as of the knife 'dripping with blood' at 59.1 – to enliven his historical account. This may seem surprising, but Livy is not writing primarily to create a document of public record, but to engage and even to entertain his readership. In this context his use of both **Direct** and **Indirect Speech** makes better sense: it does not matter that he cannot have known what was said, rather he is seeking to convey the drama of events and to give life to the characters of history. This is used especially effectively in 58.9–10: the Indirect Speech of Lucretia's family and friends gives way to her Direct Speech – she is the focus of the story, hers is the tragedy.

Livy's ability to switch between styles as his narrative moves from military strategy and politics through domestic affairs and tragedy ensures that he avoids a charge of monotony or dullness; the work remains lively and engaging, and most importantly, enjoyable to read.

A note on the text

I have largely followed the Weissenborn & Müller Teubner edition of 1898, which, being out of copyright, is readily accessible online. In a few places amendments have been made to reflect improvements of later editors and commentators.

Further reading

There follows a brief bibliography. For a more detailed introduction to the author, Walsh's *Livy* in the *Greece & Rome* New Surveys in the Classics series remains a good starting point, while his more extensive *Livy: His Historical Aims and Methods* is still very useful. Chaplin and Kraus offer a more up-to-date introduction, and many of the chapters within that volume have relevance to the selection. Morley's *Reading Ancient History* provides an entry point to ancient historiography.

On Book I, Ogilvie's *Commentary* is the most comprehensive available, but difficult to get hold of – the discussion of each episode within the Book is highly valuable to the interested reader.

Text

Weissenborn, W., Müller, H.J., *Titi Livii Ab Urbe Condita Libri Pars I: Libri I-X* (Teubner, 1898)

Commentaries

Edwards, H.J., *Livy Book I* (Cambridge, 1912)
Gould, H.E., Whiteley, J.L., *Livy Book I* (Macmillan, 1952)
Ogilvie, R.M., *Commentary on Livy Books I-V* (Oxford, 1965)

On Livy

Chaplin, J.D., Kraus, C.S., *Livy* (Oxford Readings in Classical Studies) (Oxford, 2009)

Dorey, T.A., *Livy* (Routledge & Kegan Paul, 1971)

Kraus, C.S., Woodman, A.J., *Latin Historians* (Greece & Rome – New Surveys in the Classics No. 27) (Oxford, 1997)

Miles, G.B., *Livy – Reconstructing Early Rome* (Cornell, 1995)

Walsh, P.G., *Livy: His Historical Aims and Methods* (Cambridge, 1961)

Walsh, P.G., *Livy* (Greece & Rome – New Surveys in the Classics No. 8) (Oxford, 1974)

On historiography

Morley, N., *Writing Ancient History* (Duckworth, 1999)

On the Late Republic and the Augustan Age

Beard, M. *SPQR: A History of Ancient Rome* (Profile Books, 2016)

Cooley, M., *Age of Augustus* (LACTOR, 2nd Edn 2013)

Goldsworthy, A., *Augustus: From Revolutionary to Emperor* (W&N, 2015)

Santangelo, F. *Late Republican Politics* (LACTOR, 2017)

Shotter, D.S., *The Fall of the Roman Republic* (Routledge, 2nd Edn 2005)

Shotter, D.S., *Augustus Caesar* (Routledge, 2nd Edn 2005)

On Early Rome

Cornell, T.J., *The Beginnings of Rome* (London, 1995)

Lomas, K., *The Rise of Rome* (Profile Books, 2017)

Text

In Chapters 46–52, Livy explains how Lucius Tarquinius – later called Superbus, 'the Proud' – became the Seventh King of Rome. Tullia, his second wife, urged him to take action to secure the throne by toppling her own father Servius Tullius. Tarquinius seized the throne and hurled his predecessor from the Senate House, sending men to kill him as he made his way home. Tullia, outraging all decency, drove her chariot over her father's corpse.

Tarquinius' reign is presented as being one of fear for the nobility of Rome whom he persecuted and sidelined. He looked to the neighbouring Latins for political and military support. Livy describes in Chapters 50– 51 the circumstances of a conference with the Latins, presenting Tarquinius' treatment of the Latin leader Turnus as evidence of his manipulative and base character. Chapter 52 narrates the conclusion of the treaty between the two peoples – which was very much more in the interests of the Romans than the Latins.

53. nec, ut iniustus in pace rex, ita dux belli pravus fuit; quin ea arte aequasset superiores reges, ni degeneratum in aliis huic quoque decori offecisset. is primus Volscis bellum in ducentos amplius post suam 2 aetatem annos movit Suessamque Pometiam ex iis vi cepit. ubi cum 3 dividenda praeda quadraginta talenta argenti refecisset, concepit animo eam amplitudinem Iovis templi, quae digna deum hominumque rege, quae Romano imperio, quae ipsius etiam loci maiestate esset. captivam pecuniam in aedificationem eius templi seposuit.

excepit deinde eum lentius spe bellum, quo Gabios, propinquam 4 urbem, nequiquam vi adortus, cum obsidendi quoque urbem spes pulso a moenibus adempta esset, postremo minime arte Romana, fraude ac dolo, adgressus est. nam cum velut posito bello fundamentis 5 templi iaciendis aliisque urbanis operibus intentum se esse simularet, Sextus filius eius, qui minimus ex tribus erat, transfugit ex composito Gabios, patris in se saevitiam intolerabilem conquerens: iam ab 6 alienis in suos vertisse superbiam, et liberorum quoque eum frequentiae taedere, ut quam in curia solitudinem fecerit domi quoque faciat, ne quam stirpem, ne quem heredem regni relinquat. 7 se quidem inter tela et gladios patris elapsum nihil usquam sibi tutum nisi apud hostes L. Tarquinii credidisse. nam ne errarent, manere iis bellum, quod positum simuletur, et per occasionem eum incautos invasurum. quod si apud eos supplicibus locus non 8 sit, pererraturum se omne Latium Volscosque se inde et Aequos et Hernicos petiturum, donec ad eos perveniat, qui a patrum crudelibus atque impiis suppliciis tegere liberos sciant. forsitan etiam 9 ardoris aliquid ad bellum armaque se adversus superbissimum regem ac ferocissimum populum inventurum. cum, si nihil morarentur, incensus ira porro inde abiturus videretur, benigne ab Gabinis 10 excipitur. vetant mirari, si, qualis in cives, qualis in socios, talis ad ultimum in liberos esset; in se ipsum postremo saeviturum, si alia desint. sibi vero gratum adventum eius esse, futurumque credere 11 brevi, ut illo adiuvante a portis Gabinis sub Romana moenia bellum transferatur.

54. inde in consilia publica adhiberi. ubi cum de aliis rebus adsentire se veteribus Gabinis diceret, quibus eae notiores essent, ipse identidem belli auctor esse et in eo sibi praecipuam prudentiam adsumere, quod utriusque populi vires nosset sciretque invisam profecto superbiam regiam civibus esse, quam ferre ne liberi quidem potuissent. ita cum 2 sensim ad rebellandum primores Gabinorum incitaret, ipse cum promptissimis iuvenum praedatum atque in expeditiones iret et dictis factisque omnibus ad fallendum instructis vana adcresceret fides, dux ad ultimum belli legitur. ibi cum inscia multitudine, quid ageretur, 3 proelia parva inter Romam Gabiosque fierent, quibus plerumque

Gabina res superior esset, tum certatim summi infimique Gabinorum
Sex. Tarquinium dono deum sibi missum ducem credere. apud milites 4
vero obeundo pericula ac labores pariter, praedam munifice largiendo
tanta caritate esse, ut non pater Tarquinius potentior Romae quam
filius Gabiis esset. itaque postquam satis virium conlectum ad omnes 5
conatus videbat, tum ex suis unum sciscitatum Romam ad patrem
mittit quidnam se facere vellet, quandoquidem, ut omnia unus publice
Gabiis posset, ei di dedissent. huic nuntio, quia, credo, dubiae fidei 6
videbatur, nihil voce responsum est; rex velut deliberabundus in
hortum aedium transit sequente nuntio filii; ibi inambulans tacitus
summa papaverum capita dicitur baculo decussisse. interrogando 7
expectandoque responsum nuntius fessus, ut re imperfecta, redit
Gabios; quae dixerit ipse quaeque viderit, refert; seu ira seu odio seu
superbia insita ingenio nullam eum vocem emisisse. Sexto ubi, quid 8
vellet parens quidve praeciperet tacitis ambagibus, patuit, primores
civitatis criminando alios apud populum, alios sua ipsos invidia
opportunos interemit. multi palam, quidam in quibus minus speciosa
criminatio erat futura clam interfecti. patuit quibusdam volentibus 9
fuga, aut in exilium acti sunt, absentiumque bona iuxta atque
interemptorum divisui fuere. largitiones inde praedaeque; et 10
dulcedine privati commodi sensus malorum publicorum adimi,
donec orba consilio auxilioque Gabina res regi Romano sine ulla
dimicatione in manum traditur.

*In Chapters 55–56, Tarquinius, encouraged by positive omens, turned
his attention to the city of Rome, and the construction of the great
Temple of Jupiter on the Capitoline Hill, bringing in workmen from far
and wide to assist with its completion.*

56.4 haec agenti portentum terribile visum: anguis ex columna lignea 4
elapsus cum terrorem fugamque in regia fecisset, ipsius regis non tam
subito pavore perculit pectus, quam anxiis implevit curis. itaque cum 5
ad publica prodigia Etrusci tantum vates adhiberentur, hoc velut

domestico exterritus visu Delphos ad maxime inclitum in terris
oraculum mittere statuit; neque responsa sortium ulli alii committere 6
ausus duos filios per ignotas ea tempestate terras, ignotiora maria in
Graeciam misit. Titus et Arruns profecti. comes iis additus L. Iunius 7
Brutus, Tarquinia, sorore regis, natus, iuvenis longe alius ingenio,
quam cuius simulationem induerat. is cum primores civitatis, in quibus
fratrem suum, ab avunculo interfectum audisset, neque in animo suo
quicquam regi timendum neque in fortuna concupiscendum relinquere
statuit contemptuque tutus esse, ubi in iure parum praesidii esset. ergo 8
ex industria factus ad imitationem stultitiae cum se suaque praedae
esse regi sineret, Bruti quoque haud abnuit cognomen, ut sub eius
obtentu cognominis liberator ille populi Romani animus latens
opperiretur tempora sua. is tum ab Tarquiniis ductus Delphos, 9
ludibrium verius quam comes, aureum baculum inclusum corneo
cavato ad id baculo tulisse donum Apollini dicitur, per ambages
effigiem ingenii sui. quo postquam ventum est, perfectis patris 10
mandatis cupido incessit animos iuvenum sciscitandi, ad quem eorum
regnum Romanum esset venturum. ex infimo specu vocem redditam
ferunt: imperium summum Romae habebit, qui vestrum primus, o
iuvenes, osculum matri tulerit. Tarquinii, ut Sextus, qui Romae relictus 11
fuerat, ignarus responsi expersque imperii esset rem summa ope taceri
iubent; ipsi inter se, uter prior, cum Romam redisset, matri osculum
daret, sorti permittunt. Brutus alio ratus spectare Pythicam vocem, 12
velut si prolapsus cecidisset, terram osculo contigit, scilicet quod ea
communis mater omnium mortalium esset. reditum inde Romam, ubi 13
adversus Rutulos bellum summa vi parabatur.

57. Ardeam Rutuli habebant, gens ut in ea regione atque in ea aetate
divitiis praepollens. eaque ipsa causa belli fuit, quod rex Romanus
cum ipse ditari, exhaustus magnificentia publicorum operum, tum
praeda delenire popularium animos studebat, praeter aliam superbiam
regno infestos etiam, quod se in fabrorum ministeriis ac servili tam 2

diu habitos opere ab rege indignabantur. temptata res est, si primo   3
impetu capi Ardea posset. ubi id parum processit, obsidione
munitionibusque coepti premi hostes. in his stativis, ut fit longo magis   4
quam acri bello, satis liberi commeatus erant, primoribus tamen
magis quam militibus; regii quidem iuvenes interdum otium conviviis   5
comisationibusque inter se terebant. forte potantibus his apud Sex.   6
Tarquinium, ubi et Collatinus cenabat Tarquinius, Egerii filius, incidit
de uxoribus mentio; suam quisque laudare miris modis. inde certamine   7
accenso Collatinus negat verbis opus esse, paucis id quidem horis posse
sciri, quantum ceteris praestet Lucretia sua. 'quin, si vigor iuventae inest,
conscendimus equos invisimusque praesentes nostrarum ingenia? id
cuique spectatissimum sit, quod necopinato viri adventu occurrerit
oculis.' incaluerant vino; 'age sane!' omnes; citatis equis avolant Romam.
quo cum primis se intendentibus tenebris pervenissent, pergunt inde   8
Collatiam, ubi Lucretiam haudquaquam ut regias nurus, quas in   9
convivio luxuque cum aequalibus viderant tempus terentes, sed nocte
sera deditam lanae inter lucubrantes ancillas in medio aedium sedentem
inveniunt. muliebris certaminis laus penes Lucretiam fuit. adveniens
vir Tarquiniique excepti benigne; victor maritus comiter invitat regios   10
iuvenes. ibi Sex. Tarquinium mala libido Lucretiae per vim stuprandae
capit; cum forma tum spectata castitas incitat. et tum quidem ab   11
nocturno iuvenali ludo in castra redeunt.

58. paucis interiectis diebus Sex. Tarquinius inscio Collatino cum
comite uno Collatiam venit. ubi exceptus benigne ab ignaris consilii   2
cum post cenam in hospitale cubiculum deductus esset, amore ardens,
postquam satis tuta circa sopitique omnes videbantur, stricto gladio
ad dormientem Lucretiam venit sinistraque manu mulieris pectore
oppresso 'tace, Lucretia' inquit; 'Sex. Tarquinius sum; ferrum in manu
est; moriere, si emiseris vocem.' cum pavida ex somno mulier nullam   3
opem, prope mortem imminentem videret, tum Tarquinius fateri
amorem, orare, miscere precibus minas, versare in omnes partes

muliebrem animum. ubi obstinatam videbat et ne mortis quidem 4
metu inclinari, addit ad metum dedecus: cum mortua iugulatum
servum nudum positurum ait, ut in sordido adulterio necata dicatur.
quo terrore cum vicisset obstinatam pudicitiam velut victrix libido 5
profectusque inde Tarquinius ferox expugnato decore muliebri esset,
Lucretia maesta tanto malo nuntium Romam eundem ad patrem
Ardeamque ad virum mittit, ut cum singulis fidelibus amicis veniant;
ita facto maturatoque opus esse; rem atrocem incidisse. Sp. Lucretius 6
cum P. Valerio Volesi filio, Collatinus cum L. Iunio Bruto venit, cum
quo forte Romam rediens ab nuntio uxoris erat conventus. Lucretiam
sedentem maestam in cubiculo inveniunt. adventu suorum lacrimae 7
obortae quaerentique viro 'satin salve?' 'minime' inquit; 'quid enim
salvi est mulieri amissa pudicitia? vestigia viri alieni, Collatine, in
lecto sunt tuo; ceterum corpus est tantum violatum, animus insons;
mors testis erit. sed date dexteras fidemque haud impune adultero
fore. Sex. est Tarquinius, qui hostis pro hospite priore nocte vi armatus 8
mihi sibique, si vos viri estis, pestiferum hinc abstulit gaudium.' dant 9
ordine omnes fidem; consolantur aegram animi avertendo noxam ab
coacta in auctorem delicti: mentem peccare, non corpus, et unde
consilium afuerit, culpam abesse. 'vos' inquit 'videritis, quid illi 10
debeatur; ego me etsi peccato absolvo, supplicio non libero; nec ulla
deinde impudica Lucretiae exemplo vivet.' cultrum, quem sub veste 11
abditum habebat, eum in corde defigit prolapsaque in vulnus
moribunda cecidit. conclamat vir paterque. 12

59. Brutus illis luctu occupatis cultrum ex vulnere Lucretiae extractum
manantem cruore prae se tenens, 'per hunc' inquit 'castissimum ante
regiam iniuriam sanguinem iuro vosque, dii, testes facio me L.
Tarquinium Superbum cum scelerata coniuge et omni liberorum
stirpe ferro, igni, quacumque dehinc vi possim, exsecuturum, nec illos
nec alium quemquam regnare Romae passurum.' cultrum deinde
Collatino tradit, inde Lucretio ac Valerio, stupentibus miraculo rei, 2

unde novum in Bruti pectore ingenium. ut praeceptum erat, iurant; totique ab luctu versi in iram, Brutum iam inde ad expugnandum regnum vocantem sequuntur ducem.

elatum domo Lucretiae corpus in forum deferunt concientque 3 miraculo, ut fit, rei novae atque indignitate homines. pro se quisque scelus regium ac vim queruntur. movet cum patris maestitia, tum 4 Brutus castigator lacrimarum atque inertium querellarum auctorque, quod viros, quod Romanos deceret, arma capiendi adversus hostilia ausos. ferocissimus quisque iuvenum cum armis voluntarius adest; 5 sequitur et cetera iuventus. inde praesidio relicto Collatiae ad portas custodibusque datis, ne quis eum motum regibus nuntiaret, ceteri armati duce Bruto Romam profecti. ubi eo ventum est, quacumque incedit armata multitudo, pavorem ac tumultum facit; rursus ubi 6 anteire primores civitatis vident, quidquid sit, haud temere esse rentur. nec minorem motum animorum Romae tam atrox res facit, quam 7 Collatiae fecerat. ergo ex omnibus locis urbis in forum curritur. quo simul ventum est, praeco ad tribunum Celerum, in quo tum magistratu forte Brutus erat, populum advocavit. ibi oratio habita nequaquam eius 8 pectoris ingeniique, quod simulatum ad eam diem fuerat, de vi ac libidine Sex. Tarquinii, de stupro infando Lucretiae et miserabili caede, de orbitate Tricipitini, cui morte filiae causa mortis indignior ac miserabilior esset. addita superbia ipsius regis miseriaeque et labores 9 plebis in fossas cloacasque exhauriendas demersae; Romanos homines, victores omnium circa populorum, opifices ac lapicidas pro bellatoribus factos. indigna Servi Tulli regis memorata caedes et invecta corpori 10 patris nefando vehiculo filia, invocatique ultores parentum dii. his atrocioribusque, credo, aliis, quae praesens rerum indignitas 11 haudquaquam relatu scriptoribus facilia subiecit, memoratis incensam multitudinem perpulit, ut imperium regi abrogaret exsulesque esse iuberet L. Tarquinium cum coniuge ac liberis. ipse iunioribus, qui ultro 12 nomina dabant, lectis armatisque ad concitandum inde adversus

regem exercitum Ardeam in castra est profectus; imperium in urbe
Lucretio, praefecto urbis iam ante ab rege instituto, relinquit. inter hunc 13
tumultum Tullia domo profugit exsecrantibus, quacumque incedebat,
invocantibusque parentum furias viris mulieribusque.

60. harum rerum nuntiis in castra perlatis cum re nova trepidus rex
pergeret Romam ad comprimendos motus, flexit viam Brutus –
senserat enim adventum – ne obvius fieret; eodemque fere tempore
diversis itineribus Brutus Ardeam, Tarquinius Romam venerunt.
Tarquinio clausae portae exsiliumque indictum: liberatorem urbis 2
laeta castra accepere, exactique inde liberi regis. duo patrem secuti
sunt, qui exsulatum Caere in Etruscos ierunt. Sex. Tarquinius Gabios
tamquam in suum regnum profectus ab ultoribus veterum simultatium,
quas sibi ipse caedibus rapinisque conciverat, est interfectus.

L. Tarquinius Superbus regnavit annos quinque et viginti. regnatum 3
Romae ab condita urbe ad liberatam annos ducentos quadraginta
quattuor. duo consules inde comitiis centuriatis a praefecto urbis ex
commentariis Servi Tulli creati sunt, L. Iunius Brutus et L. Tarquinius
Collatinus.

Commentary Notes

In Chapters 46–52, Livy explains how Lucius Tarquinius – later called Superbus, 'the Proud' – became the Seventh King of Rome. Tullia, his second wife, urged him to take action to secure the throne by toppling her own father Servius Tullius. Tarquinius seized the throne and hurled his predecessor from the Senate House, sending men to kill him as he made his way home. Tullia, outraging all decency, drove her chariot over her father's corpse.

Tarquinius' reign is presented as being one of fear for the nobility of Rome whom he persecuted and sidelined. He looked to the neighbouring Latins for political and military support. Livy describes in Chapters 50– 51 the circumstances of a conference with the Latins, presenting Tarquinius' treatment of the Latin leader Turnus as evidence of his manipulative and base character. Chapter 52 narrates the conclusion of the treaty between the two peoples – which was very much more in the interests of the Romans than the Latins.

Chapter 53

53.1

nec ut ... ita ... fuit: nec is taken with the second part of the statement rather than the first, although the verb is used in both – 'as unjust as the king was in peace, he was not so depraved in war'. The correlatives **ut** and **ita** establish the contrasting sides of Tarquinius' character.

iniustus in pace rex: a concise summary of what Livy has laid out regarding the domestic rule of Lucius Tarquinius Superbus, Rome's seventh king, in Chapters 49–52, before he turns to military matters; that transition is elegantly signposted by the chiasmus **pace rex . . . dux belli** (the structure ABBA: peace – Tarquinius as king – Tarquinius as general – war).

belli: locative – 'in war'.

quin: **quin** is a difficult word; on its use with the Subjunctive, see Morwood, *Latin Grammar*, 130–1. Here, however, translate simply 'in fact'; in this sense we would expect the indicative – the Subjunctives that follow have a different purpose.

aequasset . . . offecisset: Conditional Subjunctives – 'he would have . . . had not . . .'. **aequasset** is a shortened form of *aequavisset*.

superiores reges: the comparative *superior* is here used in a temporal sense – 'former' or 'earlier'. Tarquinius Superbus was the seventh and final king of Rome, but in the context of Livy's account, *superior* also suggests that he was the worst of the seven.

ni: for *nisi*.

degeneratum in aliis: the neuter of the Perfect Passive Participle used as a noun – 'his degeneracy in other matters' is the subject of **offecisset**. On Tarquinius' degeneracies, see the Introduction and Chapters 46–52.

huic . . . decori: dative – *officio* takes the dative.

53.2

is primus: 'He was the first who . . .'.

Volscis: dative – 'against the Volsci'. The Volsci were an Italian tribe living in the hill country to the south of Latium.

in ducentos . . . annos: '[which lasted] for two hundred years . . .'. A simplification of the relationship between Rome and the Volsci –

there were certainly periods of peace and cooperation over the course of the next two centuries.

Suessamque Pometiam ex iis vi cepit: the simplicity of this clause suggests it is seen as a highlight of Tarquinius' military success. This is emphasized by the choice of words: they took the city **vi** 'by force' – it was no easy task, but that he was nevertheless successful. Suessa Pometia was an ancient and important city of Latium of which no trace remained by the Classical period.

53.3

ubi: 'there', i.e. at Suessa Pometia.

dividenda praeda: ablative – 'from the plunder that was to be divided up'. The gerundive suggests that, on the sack of the city, the valuables had been gathered up and were then apportioned to each man, perhaps according to his status.

quadraginta talenta argenti: A talent was 100 Roman pounds in weight, about 33 kg. Tarquinius' bounty therefore amounted to around 1.3 tonnes of silver – which would cost you about half a million pounds at current prices.

concepit animo: 'he conceived in his mind', or perhaps, 'he had a plan for . . .'.

eam amplitudinem Iovis templi: literally, 'that grandeur of a temple of Jupiter', but better taken as 'a temple of Jupiter of such grandeur'.

What follows is a Tricolon, each element beginning **quae**. This Tricolon emphasizes just how satisfyingly worthy the temple that Tarquinius proposed to build was to the god, to the state and to its situation.

quae digna . . . esset: each element of the Tricolon is best taken as a relative result clause requiring that both **digna** and **esset** be supplied in each, 'that it would be worthy of . . .'; **quae** refers back to **amplitudinem**: it is the sheer size of the temple that is under consideration.

deum hominumque rege: Jupiter.

in aedificationem: 'for the building . . .'.

53.4

excepit . . . bellum: **bellum** needs to be taken as the subject of this clause – 'war took hold of him', we might say 'bogged him down'. Having 'war' as the subject gives a sense of events being less under Tarquinius' control and instead taking their own course; the verb promoted to the start of the sentence adds further emphasis.

lentius spe: the neuter comparative adjective, agreeing with **bellum**, followed by the Ablative of Comparison – 'more tedious than hoped'.

quo: 'in which' – Livy is going to give details of the **bellum** immediately.

The length of the next three clauses seems intended to convey the sense that this was a war that went on far longer than it should have done, while the shifting subject – first Tarquinius, then the hope of a siege, and finally Tarquinius again – suggests the to and fro of warfare.

Gabios, propinquam urbem: Gabii, as we are told here, was an ancient city near Rome – in fact about 11 miles to the east. For reasons unknown, it had rebelled from Roman dominion, and Tarquinius therefore undertook this war to regain control over it.

obsidendi urbem spes: **obsidendi** is the genitive of the gerund – 'hope *of besieging*'.

pulso a moenibus: **pulso** is dative in agreement with *ei* to be understood; this phrase depends on **adempta esset**: it was taken away from 'him as he was driven from the walls'.

minime arte Romana: 'by a method that was in no way Roman': **minime** is adverbial. The ablative **arte Romana** stands in contrast to the **vi** of earlier in the sentence.

fraude ac dolo: a pair of ablatives, picking up on and defining **minime arte Romana** as being the use of 'deceit and trickery' to achieve a military objective. The tautology ensures that the reader is in no doubt as to the moral judgement being made by Livy against such tactics: we are to understand that Roman good faith was proverbial, and such tactics were beneath them.

53.5

cum . . . simularet: an effective Temporal Clause explaining the cover that Tarquinius provided for his son's actions in Gabii.

velut posito bello: 'as if he had given up on the war'.

fundamentis ... iaciendis ... operibus: datives dependent on **intentum**.

Sextus, filius eius, qui minimus ex tribus erat: Tarquinius' other two sons, Titus and Arruns will be mentioned in Chapter 56; that Sextus is the youngest makes this passage more dramatic.

ex composito: 'by a prearranged plan'.

conquerens: 'complaining bitterly' governs both the direct object – his father's savagery towards him – and the oratio obliqua that follows.

53.6

vertisse superbiam: the clauses that follow to the end of 53.9 are an example of extended Indirect Speech or oratio obliqua – principal clauses are Indirect Statements, and all subordinate clauses are in the

Subjunctive. We need to understand that Sextus is speaking about his father: 'He said that he had turned his arrogance . . .'.

ut quam in curia solitudinem fecerit domi quoque faciat: a Purpose Clause – translate in the order *ut faciat domi quoque solitudinem quam in curia fecerit.*

ne quam stirpem, ne quem heredem regni reliquat: a further Purpose Clause – the repetition emphasizes Tarquinius' alleged aim of obliterating all heirs and successors.

53.7

se . . . credisse: 'He told them that he believed . . .'.

inter tela et gladios patris elapsum: describing his own flight in such poetic terms builds up the pathos that Sextus is aiming to elicit from the people of Gabii.

ne errarent: 'Let them not be mistaken . . .'.

bellum, quod positum simularetur: Livy consciously echoes his earlier description of the deception plan.

eum . . . invasurum: *esse* is required to complete the Future Active Infinitive – 'that he (Tarquinius) would attack . . .'.

53.8

quod si: 'But if . . .'.

apud eos supplicibus locus non sit: Sextus appeals to a traditional sense of duty towards suppliants who were expected – under divine protection – to be received and supported by those they appealed to.

pererraturum se . . . se . . . petiturum: again, supply *esse* to complete the Future Active Infinitives.

Volscosque … Aequos et Hernicos: the Volsci, Aequi and Hernici were other Latin tribes who might be willing to offer their protection.

ad eos … qui … tegere … sciant: 'to those who knew (how) to protect …'.

suppliciis: from *supplicium*, a purposeful echo of **supplicibus** from *supplex* to elicit pathos for his sufferings.

53.9

ardoris aliquid: 'some enthusiasm' – a Partitive Genitive.

ad bellum armaque: Sextus now offers the prospect that he wishes to help his protectors – whoever they might be – to fight back against Tarquinius.

se … inventurum: again, supply *esse*.

superbissimum regem: Tarquinius Superbus – Livy takes the opportunity to remind us of the defining characteristic of the final king of Rome that would be immortalized by history in the name he came to be known by.

53.10

si nihil moraretur: 'if they paid him no attention'.

incensus ira porro inde abiturus videretur: that final part of Sextus' deception is his willingness to walk away if the people of Gabii prove unresponsive.

vetant mirari: supply *eum* – 'They told him not to be amazed …'.

si, qualis … qualis … talis … esset: an effective use of Correlatives to suggest that Tarquinius' behaviour towards his children was wholly predictable.

The clauses that follow to the end of the Chapter are a further example of extended Indirect Speech.

in se ipsum . . . saeviturum: supply *esse*: 'that he would . . .'.

53.11

futurum credere . . . ut . . . transferatur: take **credere** first with *se* understood 'that they believed that . . .' followed by **futurum ut bellum transferatur**, a periphrasis of the Future Passive Infinitive clause *bellum translaturum iri* 'war would be transferred'.

Chapter 54

54.1

adhiberi: Historic Infinitive – 'he was invited'. Like the Historic Present, this is used to suggest the pace with which events took place. Livy uses a number of both the Historic Present and Historic Infinitive in this Chapter.

ubi: 'There . . .'.

quibus eae notiores essent: 'to whom those things were better known' – Sextus continues to win over the residents of Gabii by supporting their pre-existing policies in all respects except one.

ipse . . . belli auctor esse: Historic Infinitive – 'for his part he advised war . . .'.

adsumere: Historic Infinitive – (here) 'he claimed'.

quod . . . nosset sciretque . . . potuissent.: the Subjunctives are used in what amounts to Indirect Speech to show that these were the reasons Sextus himself gave for claiming a particular competency in war, rather than absolute truths.

54.2

cum sensim ... primores Gabinorum incitaret: Sextus takes his time winning over the leading – i.e. older – men of the state by words.

ad rebellandum: **ad** + Gerund, expressing Purpose, see Morwood, *Latin Grammar*, 110; the verb here effectively means 'to go back to war'.

ipse cum promptissimis iuvenum ... iret: with the younger men Sextus uses example and action to gain their support and trust.

praedatum: Supine to express Purpose, see Morwood, *Latin Grammar*, 97.

dictis factisque ... instructis: Ablative Absolute, 'as his words and deeds were designed ...'.

ad fallendum: **ad** + Gerund, expressing Purpose.

vana adcresceret fides: word order adds something to the sense here – their trust in him grew, but it was empty from the start.

dux ad ultimum belli legitur.: Sextus achieves his ultimate goal – in the end.

54.3

ibi: 'Then ...'.

inscia multitudine, quid ageretur: it is not that the people didn't know about the battles, but rather that they didn't understand that the battles were prearranged to consolidate Sextus' position in Gabii.

proelia parva: 'skirmishes'.

plerumque: the key to a convincing deceit was that the forces of Gabii were not universally victorious, but almost so.

summi infimique: 'The highest and the lowest' – i.e. all parts of Gabii society were now prepared to believe that Sextus really had changed sides.

Sex. Tarquinium dono deum sibi missum ducem: supply *esse*, an Indirect Statement – 'that Sextus Tarquinius had been sent to them as leader by gift of the gods'.

credere: Historic Infinitive – 'they believed'.

54.4

apud milites . . . tanta caritate esse: Historic Infinitive – 'He was so dear to the soldiers . . .'.

tanta caritate: Ablative of Description, see Morwood, *Latin Grammar*, 13, essentially = *tam carus*.

obeundo . . . largiendo: Gerunds in the Dative.

obeundo pericula ac labores pariter: 'for sharing equally in their dangers and toils' – he was a model commander.

praedam munifice largiendo: 'for distributing plunder generously' – and one who rewarded his men.

ut non pater Tarquinius potentior Romae quam filius Gabiis esset: an elegant Result Clause playing on the fact that father and son share a name – which we were reminded of in 54.3.

54.5

satis virium conlectum: supply *esse* 'that enough men had been collected'; **virium** is a Partitive Genitive.

sciscitatum ... quidnam se facere vellet: Supine to express Purpose – 'to ask what he wanted him to do'.

mittit: Historic Present – the passage maintains an urgent pace.

quandoquidem ... ei di dedissent: take before **ut ... posset** – 'since, indeed, the gods had granted him ...'.

ut omnia unus publice Gabiis posset: 'to be in sole command over all public affairs at Gabii'.

54.6

huic nuntio: Dative – 'to this messenger'.

quia, credo,: Livy offers his own explanation of Tarquinius' slightly strange reception of the messenger.

nihil voce responsum est: 'there was no reply by voice' – the impersonal verb gives a sense of the apparently dismissive response that the messenger received from the king ... at least in words.

sequente nuntio filii: 'with his son's messenger following him'.

summa papaverum capita: 'the topmost heads of poppies' – the stress that **summa** puts on these being the tallest of the flowers is significant in the message that the action conveys.

dicitur ... decussisse: personal construction – 'he is said to have struck off'.

54.7

interrogando expectandoque ... fessus: Ablatives of the Gerund expressing the cause of the messenger's weariness; we might say 'tired of asking and waiting for ...'.

ut re imperfecta: 'thinking his task were incomplete'.

redit: Historic Present.

refert: Historic Present, governing both the Indirect Questions that precede it, and Indirect Statement that follows.

seu ira seu odio seu superbia insita ingenio: an effective Tricolon expressing the messenger's speculation on Tarquinius' dismissive response – clearly the deception has been successful again.

nullam eum vocem emisisse.: 'that he (Tarquinius) had uttered no word'.

54.8

Sexto ubi . . . patuit: 'When it was clear to Sextus . . .'.

quid vellet parens quidve praeciperet tacitis ambagibus: apparent tautology emphasizing the means by which Sextus had worked out his father's wishes.

primores civitatis . . . interemit: corresponding with the **summa pappaverum capita**, Sextus strikes against the leaders of Gabii.

criminando: Ablative of the Gerund – 'by accusing'; Sextus' means of destroying them is to make accusations against them.

alios apud populum . . .: two groups are defined – the first are those that Sextus himself accused before the people.

alios sua ipsos invidia opportunos: the second group are those who 'made themselves suitable by their own unpopularity'.

multi palam . . . interfecti: supply *sunt*; the verb has to be used twice – the comparative length of the clauses describing the overt and secret killings is interesting.

quidam: Nominative Plural, 'certain men'.

in quibus minus speciosa criminatio erat futura: 'against whom a charge was going to be less plausible' – the meaning here is that if the individual were innocent, or might look innocent, it was better to secretly do away with him than face the embarrassment of a defence.

54.9

quibusdam volentibus: 'for some of those who wanted it' – clearly the offer of flight was not universal.

aut in exilium acti sunt: a rapid change of subject, now focusing on the people rather than the act of flight, allows Livy to suggest how many different means Sextus was employing to rid himself of opposition.

divisui fuere: literally 'were for a distribution', but better 'were available for distribution'. **divisui** is a Predicative Dative, **fuere** = *fuerunt*.

54.10

largitiones inde praedaeque: supply *erant* – 'Then there were distributions and plunder.' The concision of the clause continues the sense of pace that has been noted throughout the Chapter.

dulcedine privati commodi sensus malorum publicorum: carefully balanced phrasing 'by the charms of private gain, the sense of public ills' – word for word the one is replaced by the other.

adimi: Historic Infinitive – 'were removed'.

Gabina res regi Romano . . . in manum traditur.: 'The state of Gabii was handed over into the power of the Roman king . . .'. The use of **res** here to mean state, as found in the term *res publica* of the Roman state after the Regal Period, and its juxtaposition with **regi** are interesting in the broader context of Book I.

sine ulla dimicatione: the ancient tradition unanimously records that the Gabii came under Roman domination as the result of negotiation rather than direct conquest.

traditur: Historic Present – the Chapter concludes with the same pace that it began: all of these events happened quickly once Sextus had gained a foothold in Gabii.

In Chapters 55–56, Tarquinius turns his attention to the city of Rome, and the construction of the great Temple of Jupiter on the Capitoline Hill. The omens that surrounded its consecration were positive – Rome was destined to become a city that would rule over an empire without limits. This news encouraged Tarquinius to spend even more than he had intended on the Temple, using state funds as well as spoils of war, and summoning workmen from all parts of Etruria. As well as the Temple these workers completed the Circus seating and the Cloaca Maxima – the great sewer – which Livy tells us are works yet to be matched even in his own day. Tarquinius had to recruit additional labourers and impose this on the common people as part of their military service in order to complete his works.

Chapter 56

56.4

haec agenti: 'While he was doing these things . . ', but **agenti** is really Ablative – 'by the one doing . . .' – the agent of the Passive **visum**.

visum: supply *est* – the Passive may better be rendered Active here, 'he witnessed . . '.

anguis: the snake is given a prominent position here as the **portentum terribile** of the previous clause. Snakes were regarded as frightening omens, generally foretelling death – here, that of Tarquinius himself.

cum: 'although' – the point of this Concessive use is to show that the appearance of the snake has one impact on everyone else in the palace, and quite another on the king.

non tam ... perculit ... quam ... implevit: 'did not so much dismay ... as it did fill it ...' – again this focuses the reaction of the king very precisely.

subito pavore: 'with sudden panic' – **subito** from *subitus*.

56.5

ad publica prodigia: 'for public portents'. Portents in the public sphere, as defined by the Senate, were dealt with by one set of rules, private ones by another. It is difficult to see why the snake was considered 'private' – the *regia* was a public space in religious terms – but Tarquinius treated it as such in sending his embassy to Delphi.

tantum: 'only'.

velut domestico ... visu: there is no suggestion that Tarquinius explained his decision, only that this was the conclusion that has to be drawn from it – that he acted as if it were a private vision.

ad maxime inclitum in terris oraculum: the Oracle at Delphi had achieved pre-eminence by the end of the seventh century BC, and continued to exert influence well into the Roman period.

56.6

responsa sortium: since the replies of the Delphic Oracle were often cryptic, it was naturally important that they be faithfully reported.

ulli alii: Dative, 'to anyone else'.

duos filios: 'two of his sons' – Sextus is not sent.

per ignotas ... terras, ignotiora maria: hyperbole for dramatic effect – the route to Delphi was mainly by sea, and must have been well-known even at this early date.

Titus et Arruns: Tarquinius' two other sons.

profecti: supply *sunt.*

56.7

L. Iunius Brutus: Lucius Junius Brutus, who will play a significant role in the events that follow – Livy accordingly dedicates some time to introducing him.

iuvenis longe alius ingenio, quam cuius simulationem induerat: 'a young man very different in character to the appearance that he had assumed'.

primores civitatis, in quibus fratrem suum, ... interfectum: Indirect Statement, supply *esse*. Note that **interfectum** agrees grammatically with **fratrem** as its nearest subject, but applies equally to **primores**.

neque ... quicquam ... timendum neque ... concupiscendum: 'nothing ... to fear, nothing ... to envy' – the Gerundives agree with **quicquam**, and although Passive in Latin are better read as Active here.

statuit: governs both **relinquere** and **esse**.

contemptuque tutus: 'safe by being ignored'.

ubi ... esset.: the Subjunctive here shows that this was what Brutus himself thought to be the case.

in iure parum praesidii: 'insufficient protection in the law' – the structure of this phrase parallels **contemptuque tutus** to highlight the difference between solution and risk.

56.8

ex industria: 'deliberately'.

cum ... sineret: 'while he allowed ...'.

praedae esse regi: 'to be the king's plunder': **praedae** is a Predicative Dative, **regi**, Dative of Advantage.

Bruti ... cognomen: the name 'Brutus' means 'stupid' or 'idiot'. The implication here is that it arose as a nickname based on Brutus' assumed idiocy, and then stuck because he didn't show any objection to it. It is more probable that this was already his cognomen and that the story has been built around it.

liberator ille Romani populi animus: 'that spirit that would set free the Roman people' – Brutus will be the Liberator who frees the state from Tarquinius' tyranny ... but not yet.

tempora sua: 'its own time' – the right time would come for Brutus' true character to show itself.

56.9

is ... dicitur: Personal construction, 'He is said ...', frames a participial phrase **ductus**, and an infinitive clause **tulisse**.

Delphos: Accusative of Motion Towards without a Preposition, 'to Delphi'.

ludibrium verius quam comes: 'more as the butt of their jokes than as a companion'.

aurum baculum ... donum Apollini: the golden staff is a gift for Apollo, the god of Delphi.

inclusum corneo ... baculo: the golden staff is concealed within a wooden one, presumably to protect it on the journey.

cavato ad id: 'hollowed out for that purpose'.

per ambages effigiem: 'as an enigmatical symbol' – the gold staff hidden within a far less valuable outer sheath is taken to be just like Brutus' own concealed character.

56.10

quo: 'there', i.e. Delphi.

ventum est: Impersonal Passive, 'they arrived'.

perfectis patris mandatis: Ablative Absolute, 'once their father's orders had been carried out'. We get no answer to Tarquinius' own enquiry in Livy's account, and the focus shifts to his sons' actions at Delphi.

cupido . . . sciscitandi: 'desire to ask'; Genitive of the Gerund.

animos iuvenum: 'the hearts of the young men' – that is, presumably, of Titus and Arruns since Brutus cannot have considered the query as having any meaning for himself.

ad quem eorum . . . esset venturum: 'to which of them would come . . .' – Indirect Question, hence Subjunctive. **venturum esset** is a Periphrastic construction where Latin lacks the necessary Future Subjunctives.

ex infimo specu: 'from the depths of the cave' – the Pythian priestess who acted as mouthpiece for the god Apollo at Delphi sat over a chasm breathing in sulphurous gas.

vocem redditam ferunt: 'they say this utterance came back'.

imperium habebit: the Indicative shows that these are the actual words that were delivered by the Oracle.

qui vestrum primus: 'the first of you who'.

o iuvenes: again, apparently applicable only to Titus and Arruns.

tulerit: Future Perfect, more naturally translated as Present 'who brings'.

56.11

Tarquinii: 'the Tarquinii', i.e. Titus and Arruns.

ut Sextus . . . esset: Purpose Clause – Sextus' brothers are determined to make it back to Rome and enact the Oracle, as they understand it, before he learns of it.

expersque imperii: 'without a share in the power'.

rem summa ope taceri iubent: 'ordered that the matter be kept quiet with the greatest of care.'

iubent: Historic Present – Livy injects an excitement and urgency to this part of the story.

ipsi inter se . . . sorti permittunt.: 'They, between them, left it to fate to decide . . .'; Historic Present.

uter prior . . . matri osculum daret: Indirect Question.

Romam: Accusative of Motion Towards without a Preposition, 'to Rome'.

56.12

Brutus alio ratus spectare Pythicam vocem: 'Brutus, thinking that the Pythian utterance pointed elsewhere . . .' – i.e. that it had a different interpretation.

velut si prolapsus cecidisset: 'as if he had tripped, fell down' – it is interesting that Brutus maintains his cover as a clumsy fool, and conceals his fulfilment of the oracle by an accidental stumble.

scilicet quod: 'because, of course'.

ea communis mater: refers back to **terram**.

esset: the verb here is Subjunctive because the clause expresses Brutus' own reasoning in kissing the earth rather than an absolute fact; the rectitude of his interpretation has yet to be proven.

56.13

reditum: supply *est*, Impersonal Passive, 'they returned'.

ubi ... bellum ... parabatur: meanwhile at Rome preparations were underway for a further campaign.

Rutulos: the Rutuli, an Italian tribe whose capital was Ardea.

summa vi: perhaps implies the enthusiasm with which war was being readied rather than the violence with which it would be waged.

Chapter 57

57.1

Ardeam Rutuli habebant: Ardea was the capital of the Rutuli, standing about 25 miles south of Rome, and around 7 miles inland.

ut in ea regione atque ea tempestate: 'for that area and that time' – Livy's point is that the Rutuli would not seem especially prosperous by the standards of his own time, but were a rich target for Tarquinius.

eaque ipsa causa belli: i.e. their very wealth was the reason for the war that followed – there was no moral justification.

cum ... tum: 'not only ... but also ...'.

ditari ... delenire ... studebat.: both Infinitives are dependent on **studebat** – 'he was keen to ...'.

exhaustus magnificentia publicorum operum: Tarquinius' own resources have been depleted by the construction of the Temple of Jupiter, the seating in the Circus and the Cloaca Maxima (Chapters 55–56) on which he had spent more than originally intended.

praeda delenire popularium animos: 'with spoils to soothe the public mood' – for a moment the need to do so is left hanging; we recall Livy's record of Tarquinius' domestic injustices.

praeter aliam suberbiam regno infestos etiam: 'for in addition to his normal arrogance, they were also hostile towards the monarchy ...'. **infestos** agrees with **animos** – the people have both a general and a specific complaint to make of the king's behaviour.

57.2

quod ... indignabantur: 'because they resented' introducing an Indirect Statement.

se ... habitos: supply *esse* – '...that they had been kept ...'.

in fabrorum ministeriis ac servili ... opere: the people object to having been forced by Tarquinius to work on his temple and other works 'in the roles of craftsmen and servile labour' for such a long time – his recruitment of workmen and their resentment of the labour imposed on them was detailed at the start of Chapter 56. **fabrorum ministeriis** is balanced by **servili opere** to good effect, but the inclusion of **tam diu habitos** between the latter pair of words emphasizes by word order the length of their toil.

57.3

temptata res est: 'An attempt was made ...'.

si: 'to see if'

capi: Present Passive Infinitive from *capio*.

ubi id parum processit: the initial attempt to storm Ardea failed, and therefore Tarquinius had to resort to longer term strategies.

obsidione munitionibusque: hendiadys – 'by siege and fortifications' for 'by siege works'.

coepti premi hostes.: supply *sunt* after **coepti** – 'the enemy began to be put under pressure'. When *coepi* has a Passive Infinitive dependent on it, it is put into the Passive itself.

57.4

in his stativis: the term refers to a permanent camp, appropriate to siege warfare.

ut fit: 'as happens', or perhaps 'as is normal'.

liberi commeatus: Nominative Plural. **commeatus** is a technical term for leave of absence from the army; that it is described as **liberi** perhaps indicates a particular generosity in this respect on this occasion.

primoribus tamen magis quam militibus: this unfair distinction in freedom of movement between leaders and the men serving under them almost seems an inevitability, but here sets up the circumstances in which Sextus Tarquinius might be expected to have particular liberty despite being at war.

57.5

regii . . . iuvenes: the princes – although the narrative is going to be about Sextus, the implication is that Titus and Arruns (who have been referred to by the term **iuvenes** in Chapter 56) were also present for these parties.

quidem: picking up on the previous sentence to focus not just on the leading men, but on the three princes in particular.

otium ... terebant: 'were wearing away their leisure time' – a somewhat poetic turn of phrase preparing the reader for the way in which the characters interact in what follows.

conviviis comisationibusque: 'in banquets and drinking parties', a pleasantly alliterative phrase that seems to have been in common use in Livy's time – Cicero also uses it. The drinking is the key to understanding how things go wrong.

inter se: implies a social clique who enjoyed spending time together somewhat exclusively.

57.6

potantibus his: Ablative Absolute, 'while they were drinking' – again an emphasis on drink.

apud Sex. Tarquinium: 'with Sextus Tarquinius'. The force of **apud** here is to suggest that Sextus was the host on this occasion.

Collatinus ... Tarquinius, Egerii filius: Collatinus was the son of Egerius, a nephew of Lucius Tarquinius Priscus, the Fifth King of Rome, and so a distant relative of Sextus.

incidit de uxoribus mentio: 'discussion turned to wives' – this is not the language of narrative but of colloquial and spontaneous conversation.

suam quisque laudare: 'each praised his own' – thus the discussion starts off reasonably, but at a pace indicated by the Historic Infinitive.

miris modis.: 'in wonderful ways' – the phrase, again alliterative, seems to have had an archaic ring for the contemporary reader, appropriate to the championing of legendary wives.

57.7

certamine accenso: Ablative Absolute, 'when their contest grew heated'.

Collatinus negat: the verb governs both **opus esse** and **posse sciri**, but only carries the negative sense on the first occasion – 'Collatinus said that there was no need ... and that ...'.

verbis: Ablative with **opus esse**.

paucis ... horis: Collatia, where Lucretia was, was about 25 miles from Ardea across country, a reasonable distance to cover by horse 'in a few hours'.

id ... posse sciri: Indirect Statement, 'that it could be known'; the **id** in question is supplied by the next clause, **quantum. . .**

quantum: Adverbial Accusative, 'how much ...'.

Lucretia sua: displaced to the end of its clause, Collatinus is boasting that it is his wife, his Lucretia that is the best.

quin ... conscendimus: 'why don't we mount ...'. This use of **quin** with the Indicative is generally found only in Classical Latin in passages of heightened emotion.

si vigor iuventae inest: an implicit challenge to those he is drinking with: are they youthful enough, are they strong enough, for such a decisive action?

invisimusque praesentes: 'and see in person' – **praesentes** Nominative Plural.

nostrarum: 'of our wives'.

id ... sit: 'let that be', Jussive Subjunctive.

spectatissimum: 'the decisive proof'.

quod . . . occurrerit oculis: quod picks up **id**, 'that which meets the eyes.'

necopinato viri adventu: 'on the unexpected arrival of her husband.'

incaluerant vino: 'they had grown hot with wine' – drinking has clouded their judgement; the heat metaphor is picked up from **certamine accenso** above.

'age sane!' omnes: supply *dixerunt*; **age sane** means something like 'Come on then!'. Note the brevity of the sentences – and the omission of a verb here – which indicate the pace of their actions.

equis avolant: 'they fly on their horses' – the verb is Historic Present, the juxtaposition of the words underlines the pleasing metaphor that highlights their speed.

Romam: Accusative of Motion Towards without a Preposition, 'to Rome'.

57.8

quo: 'there'

primis se intendentibus tenebris: Ablative Absolute, 'as darkness was first deepening'; *intendo* requires a Direct Object, **se**.

pergunt inde Collatiam: Historic Present, and short clause combine to give a sense of urgent pace – they don't pause, but set out immediately again for Collatia, a distance of about another 13 miles.

57.9

ubi . . . inveniunt.: a much longer structure, but still with its verb Historic Present.

Lucretiam haudquaquam . . . tempus terentes: Lucretia is contrasted directly with the women they have already seen at Rome. Note the use of the verb *tero* – c.f. **otium . . . terebant** (57.5). It seems that everyone is wasting their time except Lucretia.

ut regias nurus, quas . . . viderant: 'like the royal daughters-in-law whom they had seen . . ', i.e. the wives of the king's sons whom we are to infer had been viewed in passing through Rome.

in convivio luxuque: c.f. **conviviis comisationibusque** (57.5) – the behaviour of the other women is far less morally upright than that of Lucretia.

sed nocte sera: 'but even though it was late at night' – Lucretia has not given herself over to partying.

deditam lanae: 'wholly given over to her wool', i.e. spinning. There is a close link in the Greco-Roman world between wool-making and feminine virtue. Lucretia, sat in her home – as the ideal wife was expected to be – and surrounded by hardworking female slaves is an ideal image of Roman womanhood.

57.10

muliebris certaminis laus: 'the honour in this contest about their wives'.

penes Lucretiam: 'with Lucretia', i.e. she won the contest.

adveniens: strictly in agreement only with **vir**, but also true of **Tarquiniique**.

excepti: supply *sunt* – both her husband and the Tarquinii were well received by Lucretia.

victor maritus: a contextually appropriate, but strange, juxtaposition that blurs the language of war and domesticity.

invitat: Historic Present.

regios iuvenes: certainly Sextus, presumably also Titus and Arruns.

mala libido . . . capit: the 'wicked lust' is the subject of the sentence, personified in this strong sentence.

Lucretiae . . . stuprandae: Gerundive in the Dative – it is a lust 'for debauching Lucretia', we might say 'a wicked lust to violate Lucretia'.

per vim: a powerful expression – Sextus intended to use force to get his way; he doesn't even see it as something that might involve consent. **per vim** also anticipates the violence which follows when Sextus does the deed.

capit: Historic Present – we are reminded that this whole episode has taken place at a terrific pace.

cum . . . tum: here, 'both . . . and . . .'.

spectata castitas: her previously 'observed chastity' is an incentive to Sextus.

57.11

ab nocturno iuvenali ludo: 'from their juvenile night-time game' – Livy concludes the Chapter recalling that this was all supposed to be just a bit of fun, but the preceding sentence has given warning of the serious consequences of their game.

redeunt: Historic Present.

Chapter 58

58.1

paucis interiectis diebus: Ablative Absolute, little more than 'a few days later'.

inscio Collatino: obvious from what follows, but here establishing the impropriety of Sextus' subsequent visit to Collatia.

58.2

ubi ... inquit: Tarquinius' arrival is described in a complicated series of clauses making up a single long sentence – everything happens in sequence in a complex and planned fashion.

ubi: 'there'.

exceptus benigne ab ignaris consilii: 'received kindly by those unaware of the plan' – the hospitality shown to Sextus stands in sharp contrast to the outrage he is planning to enact.

cum ... deductus esset: Sextus is provided with both a dinner and a suitable guestroom – his hostess is blissfully unaware of the threat, and acting with absolute propriety.

amore ardens: brief and simple, but powerfully expressed, Participial phrase reminding the reader of Sextus' 'burning' passion; note assonance.

postquam ... videbantur: Temporal Clause; Sextus doesn't act hastily, but rather waits for the rest of the household to be asleep – his passion may be blazing, but his actions are cold and calculating.

satis tuta circa sopitique omnes: 'everything around was safe enough and all were asleep.'

stricto gladio: Ablative Absolute, 'with his sword drawn'.

ad dormientem Lucretiam: Lucretia has gone to bed unaware of the threat within her home.

sinistraque manu mulieris pectore oppresso: 'with his left hand he pressed down upon the woman's breast' – his right hand, of course, is holding his sword. These two Ablative Absolutes (**stricto gladio** and **pectore oppresso**) frame the simplicity of the main clause (**ad dormientem Lucretiam venit**) to give a truly threatening image: it is a terrifying way for her to wake up.

'**tace . . . vocem**.': by contrast with the complex sentence describing Sextus' arrival and entry into Lucretia's bedroom, his words are quick and to the point, expressed in short self-contained periods.

moriere: variant Second Person Singular, for *morieris* 'you will die'.

58.3

pavida ex somno: 'startled from her sleep'.

nullam opem, prope mortem imminentem: supply *esse* – 'that there was no help, death threatening nearby . . .'.

Tarquinius fateri. . ., orare, miscere, versare: Historic Infinitives in Asyndeton – Sextus continues to speak with breathless urgency. We note a slide in his technique from a confession of love, through begging, to threatening and manipulating: this is not real love.

versare in omnes partes muliebrem animum: 'twisted her womanly mind in every direction', i.e. applied every conceivable pressure on it.

58.4

obstinatam: supply *eam . . . esse* – Indirect Statement 'that she was resolute'.

ne mortis quidem metu inclinari: again, supply *eam* – Indirect Statement 'that she was not even caused to waver by fear of death'.

addit ad metum dedecus: a very simple clause expresses Sextus' final method – he identifies what Lucretia is really afraid of, dishonour. **dedecus** is Accusative.

cum mortua: 'beside her in death'.

iugulatum servum nudum positurum: supply *esse* – 'that he would place a naked slave with his throat cut'. The anonymity of the slave contributes to the horror of the suggestion.

ut ... dicatur: Purpose Clause – 'so that it would be said'.

in sordido adulterio: the implication is that the adultery with which she would be posthumously charged would be even more dishonourable because with a slave.

necata: supply *esse* – 'that she had been killed'.

58.5

quo terrore: 'by fear of this'.

cum vicisset: Sextus Tarquinius is the subject; the language becomes martial – Sextus regards himself as a conquering hero. The imagery of this section is enhanced by strong vocabulary – **vicisset, pudicitiam, victrix, libido, expugnato, decore**.

obstinatam pudicitiam: 'stubborn modesty' – an unusual adjective to describe **pudicitiam**. Note repetition with variation of use: **obstinatam** was also used of Lucretia herself at 58.4.

velut victrix libido: 'as if lust really had won' – it is as though Sextus can pretend to himself that threats had not been necessary and she had surrendered herself willingly to him.

profectusque inde Tarquinius ... esset: also taken with **cum** – Sextus departs, the deed done.

ferox: an Adjective with both positive and negative connotations – in his own mind, Sextus is 'daring' and 'warlike', but Lucretia, and the reader, perceive him as 'brutish' and 'savage'.

expugnato decore mulieri: Ablative Absolute, continuing the military metaphor – 'once the woman's honour had been taken by storm'. The violence of a military assault, conveyed in **expugnato**, vividly suggests the brutality of Lucretia's rape. It is as much detail as Livy gives us, but in its cruel brevity it is enough.

Lucretia ... nuntium ... eundeum ... mittit: Main Clause – 'Lucretia ... sent the same message'; note Historic Present.

maesta tanto malo: 'filled with sorrow at such an evil', very effectively simplicity of expression shows the depth of Lucretia's emotions, and the horror of the rape.

Romam ... ad patrem Ardeamque ad virum: the repeated pattern of words is effective – it is exactly the same message that she sends to both her father and her husband.

ut. . .incidisse.: Lucretia's message takes the form of a Tricolon – one Indirect Command followed by two Indirect Statements. The language is formal and archaic, the clauses increasingly brief, but the third element of the Tricolon certainly has the greatest impact.

cum singulis fidelibus amicis: 'with one faithful friend each'.

ita facto maturatoque opus esse: 'that there was need for it to be done in this way, and done quickly'. The Ablative Singular of the Neuter of the Perfect Passive Participle (**facto** and **maturato**) is often found with *opus est* in place of a noun.

58.6

Sp. Lucretius: Spurius Lucretius, Lucretia's father.

P. Valerio Volesi filio: Publius Valerius, the son of Volesus.

L. Iunius Brutus: Lucius Junius Brutus, see. 56.7.

forte: the fact that Brutus happened to be travelling with Collatinus is a significant dramatic coincidence.

ab nuntio uxoris erat conventus.: 'he had been met by his wife's messenger'.

inveniunt: Historic Present.

58.7

adventu suorum: **suorum** means literally 'of her own', hence of those who would be on her side – her friends: 'at the arrival of supporters'.

lacrimae obortae: supply *sunt* – 'tears welled up'.

quaerentique viro: Dative, but effectively 'and when her husband asked her'.

'satin salve?': an old-fashioned greeting, for '*satis ne salve?*' 'Are you well enough?'

'minime' inquit: a crushingly simple response to her husband's question.

'quid . . . salvi est mulieri: 'How can a woman be well . . .'.

amissa pudicitia: Ablative Absolute, 'when her modesty is lost'. Note repetition of the important vocabulary – **pudicitia**.

vestigia viri alieni . . . in lecto sunt tuo: for this confession of the circumstances of her lost modesty Lucretia uses straightforward language. **vestigia** refers to the imprint of Sextus's body in the bed, to his trespass upon Collatinus' territory, and, of course, in a literal sense to the marks he has left behind.

ceterum: 'But'.

corpus est . . . violatum, animus insons: a strong contrast between body and mind, but also between Passive and Active.

tantum: 'only'.

mors testis erit: i.e. of the truth of what she has said.

sed date dexteras fidemque: strong Alliteration in 'd' underlines Lucretia's determination as she makes the four men give her their word.

haud impune ... fore.: supply *id*, 'the deed will not be unpunished'. **fore** for *futurum esse*.

adultero: Dative 'for the adulterer', here, in the sense of one who has violated another's marriage, rather than extra-marital lover.

58.8

Sex. est Tarquinius: 'It was Sextus Tarquinius ...'.

qui hostis pro hospite: 'who as an enemy instead of a guest' – a reminder of the hospitality that Lucretia had shown him on his arrival and of the warlike depiction of his act. The echo effect of **hostis ... hospite** supports the contrast.

priore nocte: 'last night'.

vi armatus: 'armed with force', again emphasizing the violence of the rape; the term *vis armata* was a Roman legal expression for violence committed with the use of weapons.

mihi sibique ... pestiferum hinc abstulit gaudium.: 'stole joy from here – deadly for me, and for him too ...'. **pestiferum** agrees with **gaudium**, and applies equally to **mihi** and **sibique** – Lucretia sees her own death as inevitable and hopes that his will be too.

sibique, si vos viri estis: the challenge is clear – they will only prove their manhood if they avenge her rape.

58.9

dant ordine omnes fidem: 'They all gave their word in turn.' Note brevity of the promise, promoted verb and Historic Present – events are again moving apace and with drama.

consolantur: Historic Present, again promoted to the front of its clause.

aegram animi: supply *eam*, 'she who was sick in mind'.

avertendo noxam ab coacta in auctorem delicti: 'by diverting blame from she who had been forced onto him who instigated the wrong.' **avertendo** Ablative of the Gerund.

mentem peccare, non corpus: Indirect Statement, following on from **consolantur** – 'They said that it was the mind that sinned, not the body.' The distinction between mind and body that Lucretia herself made in 58.7 is repeated by her supporters – if her mind is innocent, then so is she.

et unde consilium afuerit, culpam abesse: further Indirect Speech – 'and that where there has been no intent, there is no blame.'

58.10

vos ... videritis: Future Perfect – 'You will determine ...'. Lucretia uses Direct Speech – in contrast with the Indirect Speech which precedes it.

vos ... ego me: note emphatic position of personal pronouns in both clauses.

quid illi debeatur: Indirect Question – 'what is owed to that man'.

nec ulla deinde impudica Lucretiae exemplo vivet: 'let no unchaste woman ever live on the precedent of Lucretia.' She is clear that by subjecting herself to the death penalty, her circumstances can never be used as an excuse to escape punishment for unchastity – even though no blame attaches itself to her in her rape. **vivet** – Present Subjunctive.

58.11

cultrum eum: 'that knife'.

quem sub veste abditum habebat: 'which she had concealed beneath her robe' – Lucretia's suicide has been planned before the arrival of the four men.

in corde defigit: Historic Present – 'she plunged into her heart'.

prolapsaque in vulnus: she gracefully slips forwards over the wound.

moribunda: a stark adjective – there is nothing that can be done: she is dying.

58.12

conclamat vir paterque.: a short sentence full of pathos; note Historic Present and the verb at the start for emphasis and drama – 'Her husband cried out, and so did her father.'

Chapter 59

59.1

Brutus: emphatic position – the attention now shifts to him.

illis luctu occupatis: Ablative Absolute, 'while they were busy with their grief' – presumably Lucretia's husband and father.

cultrum . . . extractum: Perfect Passive Participle, better translated as a separate finite verb – 'drew the knife out . . . and'.

manentem cruore prae se tenens: dramatically graphic details, reminiscent of Cicero's description of the later Brutus drawing the bloodied knife from Caesar's corpse – on the comparison, and its risks, see Introduction.

per hunc . . . sanguinem: Brutus' oath is powerfully sworn by Lucretia's own blood.

castissimum ante regiam iniuriam: describing **sanguinem** – 'most chaste until the prince defiled it'.

vosque, dii, testes facio: 'and I make you, gods, my witnesses' – invoking the gods is a powerful, traditional and legally-framed formula by which Brutus binds himself to the fulfilment of his oath.

me . . . exsecuturum: supply *esse*, the first of two Indirect Statements – 'that I shall punish . . .'.

L. Tarquinium Superbum: in its immediate context somewhat surprisingly, but in wider terms understandably, Brutus turns his anger on Tarquinius the father rather than Sextus the son who had actually committed the rape. In effect the rape of Lucretia is seized upon at once by Brutus to overthrow a disliked monarch and monarchy.

ferro, igni, quacumque dehinc vim possim: a Tricolon with Asyndeton – Brutus pledges to use 'sword, fire and ultimately whatever violence I can' to overthrow Tarquinius and his whole family.

nec . . . passurum.: supply both *me* and *esse*, the second Indirect Statement – 'and that I shall not allow . . .'.

Romae: Locative, 'at Rome'.

59.2

cultrum . . . Collatino tradit, inde Lucretio ac Valerio: Brutus hands the knife around so that the others can swear the same oath as he – as is made clear in the next sentence; note Historic Present.

stupentibus miraculo rei: referring to all three men, 'who were amazed at the wonder of the matter . . .'.

unde novum in Bruti pectore ingenium: what they were amazed at – 'where this new character had come from in Brutus' heart'. Until that moment, like everyone else, they had considered him dull and foolish.

ut praeceptum erat, iurant: 'as had been instructed, they swore', note Historic Present.

totique ab luctu versi in iram: 'and altogether turned from grief to anger'.

iam inde: 'from that very moment'.

ad expungnandum regnum: ad + Gerund, here Gerundive by Attraction, expressing Purpose – 'to take the kingdom by assault'. *expugno* was memorably the verb used of Sextus' rape of Lucretia at 58.5, and its repetition here is deliberate and powerful.

sequuntur: Historic Present.

ducem.: 'as leader' – emphatic position at the end of the sentence; this was not a predictable role for Brutus to adopt, but by their unhesitating support he has clearly won it.

59.3

elatum domo Lucretiae corpus: take **elatum** as if a Finite Verb – 'They carried Lucretia's body out of the house, and . . .'. *effero* is the technical term for carrying out a body for a funeral.

in forum deferunt: note Historic Present; the body is taken into the **forum** – not just a market-place but also an important town-centre – in Collatia.

concientque: Historic Present; the object of the verb is **homines**. Note juxtaposition of **deferunt concientque** – the first act leads seamlessly into its immediate consequence.

miraculo . . . atque indignitate: 'in wonder . . . and indignation.' The men of Collatia are both surprised but also immediately join in anger at the death of Lucretia.

ut fit: 'as happens', or perhaps 'as is normal', see 57.4.

rei novae: 'with something new'.

pro se quisque . . . queruntur: 'each complained on their own behalf about . . '; Historic Present.

scelus regium ac vim: the rebellion is already gaining momentum, as each man considers himself to have been wronged by the royal household.

59.4

movet: supply *eos* as object; note Historic Present, and verb at start of sentence for emphasis.

cum . . . tum: 'not only . . . but also'.

Brutus castigator . . . auctorque: 'Brutus who chastised them for . . . and encouraged them . . '.

inertium querellarum: Genitive Plural – 'useless complaints'.

quod viros, quod Romanos deceret,: 'what was right for men, what was right for Romans' – Brutus appeals to their sense of pride in their identity. The Subjunctive in virtual Indirect Speech – Livy is capturing Brutus' own argument.

arma capiendi: take with **auctor** – 'encouraged them to take up arms'. **capiendi** is Genitive of the Gerund.

adversus hostilia ausos: 'against those that dared hostile acts'.

59.5

ferocissimus quisque iuvenum: 'each of the boldest of the young men'.

adest; sequitur: Historic Presents, juxtaposed – the bravest are there straight away, but the rest aren't far behind; again, events have a rapid pace to them.

sequitur et cetera iuventus: 'the rest of the youth followed too'; significant emphasis is placed in this passage on the response of the youth.

praesidio relicto: Ablative Absolute; they are not leaving Collatia itself undefended.

custodibusque datis: Ablative Absolute; these guards have a separate duty – to protect the rebels from betrayal.

ne quis … nuntiaret: negative Purpose Clause – 'so that no one reported …'.

eum motum: 'that movement', here 'the uprising'.

regibus: an interesting plural 'to the rulers', perhaps intended 'to the royal family'.

duce Bruto: Ablative Absolute, 'with Brutus as their leader'.

profecti: supply *sunt*.

59.6

ventum est: Impersonal Passive – 'they arrived'.

quacumque incedit armata multitudo: 'wherever the armed horde went'. **incedit** and **facit** – Historic Presents.

anteire primores civitatis: Indirect Statement – 'that it was the leading men of the state who were at the front'.

vident: supply, perhaps, *cives* as subject; Historic Present.

quidquid sit, haud temere esse rentur.: 'they thought that, whatever it was, it wasn't going to be without a good reason.'

59.7

nec minorem motum animorum: 'no less resentment', literally, 'no less movement of minds'.

tam atrox res: i.e. the rape and subsequent death of Lucretia.

Romae: Locative, 'at Rome'.

facit: Historic Present.

Collatiae: Locative, 'at Collatia'.

in forum curritur: Impersonal Passive, 'there was a rush to the Forum' – these Impersonal Passives give a sense that all of Rome was on the move while at the same time allowing the focus to remain on Brutus. Note Historic Present.

ventum est: Impersonal Passive, as in 59.6.

praeco . . . populum advocavit: 'a herald drew the people's attention'.

ad tribunum Celerum: 'to the Tribune of the Celeres'; the Celeres were the royal bodyguard – a permanent armed force – who were led by a Tribune.

in quo tum magistratu forte Brutus erat: holding this office gave Brutus the right to address the people, convenient to the narrative. It seems unlikely – given the contempt in which Brutus had been held – that such an important, if any, magistracy would be entrusted to him, and Cicero's account of the foundation of the Republic makes him only a private citizen.

59.8

oratio habita: supply *est* – perhaps best translated as if Active, 'he delivered a speech'.

nequaquam eius pectoris ingeniique: 'completely different from the sentiment and character . . .'. The *pectus* was the seat of the emotions, in English, 'the heart'; it was last used at 58.2 in the physical sense of Lucretia's breast.

quod simulatum . . . fuerat: 'which he had feigned'.

de vi ac libidine . . . de strupro . . . de orbitate: a notable Tricolon echoing the rhetorical force of Brutus' speech. Again we note the use of very powerful vocabulary – especially **de stupro infando** 'of the unspeakable defilement'.

de orbitate Tricipitini: i.e. Lucius Spurius Tricipitinus, Lucretia's father, named at 58.6 without this cognomen.

cui morte filiae causa mortis indignior ac miserabilior esset: 'for whom the cause of his daughter's death had been more unworthy and more pitiable than the death itself.' Note the chiastic word order **morte filiae causa mortis**; **morte filiae** 'the death of his daughter' as an Ablative of Comparison is brought forward in the clause for emphasis.

59.9

addita superbia: supply *est* – as in the previous sentence, it may be best to read this as Active, 'Brutus also mentioned the arrogance . . .'.

ipsius regis: i.e. Tarquinius Superbus.

miseriaeque et labores: further subjects taken with **addita** *est*.

plebis . . . demersae: 'of the people sent underground'.

in fossas cloacasque exhauriendas: 'to drain the ditches and sewers' – Gerundive, here with **in** rather than *ad*, but still expressing Purpose. The construction of the Great Sewer, and the discontent it had caused, was mentioned in Chapter 56.

Romanos homines . . . factos: supply *esse* – Indirect Statement. 'He said that Roman men . . . had been made . . .'.

victores omnium circa populorum: what Romans had achieved previously, and what Brutus considered should be their role.

opifices ac lapicidas: what Tarquinius had made them instead: tradesmen, viewed as very much inferior to warriors.

59.10

indigna . . . memorata caedes: supply *est* – again, better read as Active, 'He recalled the undeserved slaughter . . .'.

Servi Tulli regis: Servius Tullius, the Sixth King of Rome, who had been brutally murdered when Tarquinius seized the throne – see Chapter 48.

invecta corpori patris nefando vehiculo filia: a further subject of **memorata** *est* – 'the daughter carried in her wicked chariot over her father's body'. Tullia, the daughter of Servius Tullis, but the wife of Tarquinius, is said to have deliberately had her chariot driven over her father's corpse. This was an afront to decency and divine law – hence the chariot can accurately be described as **nefando**, even if that adjective would be better applied to Tullia herself.

invocatique ultores parentum dii.: supply *sunt*, still best taken Active – 'and he called upon the gods that avenge parents.'

59.11

his atrocibusque, credo, aliis ... memoratis: Ablative Absolute – 'When these and, I believe, other more terrible things had been mentioned ...'. With **credo** Livy enters the narrative personally to express an opinion.

praesens rerum indignitas ... subiecit: 'which the outrage of the moment at events suggested'.

haudquaquam relatu scriptoribus facilia: 'not at all easy for writers to describe'. By *scriptores* Livy means historians, and so himself; **relatu** Dative of the Supine. The recusatio that Livy achieves in this phrase is highly effective: neither he as a historian, nor we as a reader, can fully express the hostility of the moment – but we can imagine it.

ut ... abrogaret ... iuberet: a pair of Purpose Clauses, or perhaps Indirect Commands – it depends how forcefully we think Brutus drove the **incensam multitudinem** 'the fired-up crowd'.

imperium regi abrogaret: the term *abrogare* was a technical one for removing a magistrate's imperium – a technical grant of power – in the Republican period; it is appropriate here as the removal of the king's power will establish the Republic.

exsulesque esse iuberet L. Tarquinium cum coniuge ac liberis: **exsules** is plural in reference to Lucius Tarquinius Superbus, his wife and his children, although the grammar at the end of the clause is different – the focus is on Tarquinius himself, but his whole family are to be exiled with him. After the horrors that Brutus has mentioned, exile seems a compassionate outcome for Tarquinius.

59.12

ipse . . . profectus: supply *est*; i.e. Brutus.

iunioribus . . . lectis armatis: Ablative Absolute – 'once the Juniors . . . had been enrolled and armed'. *iuniores* were a classification of Roman citizens liable for military service.

qui ultro nomina dabant: i.e. they volunteered at this moment.

ad concitandum inde adversum regem exercitum: 'to stir up the army there against the king' – **ad** + Gerund, here Gerundive by Attraction, expressing Purpose. Brutus recognized the need to have the military on side if the revolution were to be successful.

imperium in urbe Lucretio . . . relinquit. 'He left power in the city to Lucretius . . .' – note Historic Present.

praefecto urbis iam ante ab rege instituto: 'who had already been installed as Prefect of the City by the king.' The role of *praefectus urbis* had been revived by Julius Caesar, and was used consistently by Augustus under whom Livy was writing; it certainly had Republican precedent.

59.13

inter hunc tumultum: 'During this upheaval . . .'.

Tullia: mentioned above, the wife of Tarquinius.

exsecrantibus . . . invocantibus . . . viris mulieribusque.: Ablative Absolute – 'while men and women cursed her . . . and called upon . . .'.

quacumque incedebat: 'wherever she went'.

parentum furias: 'the spirits that avenge crimes against parents'.

Chapter 60

60.1

nuntiis ... perlatis: Ablative Absolute – 'when news had been brought'.

cum ... rex pergeret: although **cum** here is followed by an Ablative, that is coincidental; take with the Subjunctive **pergeret** – 'while ...'.

re nova trepidus: describing the king's reaction – 'nervous at the strange turn of events' – and his reasons for hastening to Rome.

Romam: Accusative of Motion Towards without a Preposition – 'to Rome'.

ad comprimendos motus: **ad** + Gerund, here Gerundive by Attraction, expressing Purpose – 'to crush the uprising'. **motus**, literally 'the movement' as at 59.5.

flexit viam Brutus: Main Clause – 'Brutus took a circuitous route ...'.

ne obviam fieret: Negative Purpose Clause – 'so as not to meet him'.

eodemque fere tempore: Ablative of Time When – 'at almost the same time'.

diversis itinieribus: 'by differing routes'.

Brutus Ardeam: supply *venerunt*. Note the deliberate parallel in word order between this and the clause that immediately follows: **Tarquinius Romam venerunt**. Both **Ardeam** and **Romam** – Accusative of Motion towards without a Preposition.

60.2

Tarqinio: Dative of Disadvantage.

clausae: supply *sunt*.

exsiliumque indictum: supply *est*.

liberatorem: Livy has brought the word forward in the sentence to create a parallel structure with **Tarquino** preceding it. The reception of Tarquinius at Rome and Brutus in the camp at Ardea are thereby contrasted effectively.

laeta castra: **laeta** is an Adjective, but perhaps better rendered as 'the camp happily ...'.

accepere: variant Third Person Plural in the Perfect Tense, for *acceperunt* 'received' – the camp (Neuter Plural) is the subject.

exactique: supply *sunt*.

liberi regis: Titus, Arruns and Sextus.

duo: the next sentence makes it clear that this refers to Titus and Arruns.

exsulatum: Supine to express Purpose after the Verb of Motion **ierunt**, see Morwood, *Latin Grammar*, 97 – 'to be exiles'.

Caere in Etruscos: 'at Caere among the Etruscans' – Caere was about 25 miles from Rome, and seems to have been the ancestral home of the Tarquinii. The discovery in 1850 of a tomb dating to the fifth to third centuries BC appears to confirm the familial association.

Gabios ... profectus: 'having set out for Gabii' – Accusative of Motion Towards without a Preposition.

tamquam in suum regnum: it will be recalled that in Chapters 53 and 54, Sextus Tarquinius had made Gabii loyal to him, and it is natural that he sought refuge, and perhaps a base of operations there.

ab ultoribus veterum simultatium: 'by avengers of old feuds' – although the following clause gives some indication of the nature of the feuds, the avengers themselves are anonymous – we are intended to understand that Sextus Tarquinius had many enemies.

caedibus rapinisque: 'by murders and thefts' – similarly the plurals suggest that Sextus had a history of such behaviour. *rapina* does not imply rape, but only the act of taking what is not your own; nevertheless, the phrase here must be intended to recall the rape and death of Lucretia.

est interfectus. The inversion of the elements of the verb (we expect *interfectus est*) gives a satisfying finality to Livy's account of Sextus Tarquinius.

60.3

L. Tarquinius Superbus regnavit annos quinque et viginti: this echoes a formula that Livy has applied to mark the closure of several reigns in Book I.

regnatum: supply *est* – Impersonal Passive, 'there were kings'.

Romae: Locative – 'at Rome'.

ab condita urbe: 'from the foundation of the city', i.e. by Romulus in 753 BC. Livy's history has the title *ab Urbe Condita* – indicative of the content of its early books, but also of its projected scale.

ad libertatam: 'to its liberation', i.e. the removal of Tarquinius Superbus by Brutus and the subsequent establishment of the Republic two hundred and forty-four years later in 509 BC. **libertatam** agrees with *urbem* understood.

duo consules: Livy is factually incorrect here – the Republic was set up with two Praetors taking over from the kings; the creation of

Consuls in this function came later. The error is unimportant, however: the Consulship – and especially its binary nature – was at the heart of Republican government, and had huge political significance when Livy was composing his History.

comitiis centuriatis: 'at the assembly by centuries' – likewise it is unlikely that the Centuriate Assembly existed at this early date.

a praefecto urbis: which was, of course, Lucretius, Lucretia's father.

ex commentariis Servi Tulli: 'according to the commentaries of Servius Tullius' – to be taken with **creati sunt**. Servius Tullius seems to have formalized and regulated the process of election – Livy's point here is that the election of the first Consuls, if we are to call them that, followed established process as already defined at that time: it was legitimate.

creati sunt: 'were elected'.

Vocabulary

While there is no Defined Vocabulary List for A-Level, words in the OCR Defined Vocabulary List for AS are marked with * so that students can quickly see the vocabulary with which they should be particularly familiar.

* a, ab (+ abl.)	by, from
abdo, abdere, abdidi, abditum	conceal, hide away
abeo, abire, abi(v)i	go away
abnuo, abnuere, abnui	refuse
abrogo, -are, -avi, -atum	take away
absolvo, absolvere, absolve, absolutum	acquit, absolve
* absum, abesse, afui	be absent, be away, be distant
* ac, atque	and
accendo, accendere, accendi, accensum	set on fire, inflame
* accipio, accipere, accepi, acceptum	receive
* acer, acris, acre	sharp, keen; fierce, violent
* ad (+ acc.)	to, towards; for
ad ultimum	at last, finally, in the end
adcresco, -ere, -crevi, -cretum	grow, increase
* addo, addere, addidi, additum	add,
adgredior, -gredi, -gressus sum	attack
adhibeo, -ere, adhibui, adhibitum	invite, apply, employ
* adimo, adimere, ademi, ademptum	take away, remove
* adiuvo, adiuvare, adiuvi, adiutum	help
adorior, -oriri, -ortus sum	attack
adsentire, adsentire, adsensi, adsensum	agree
* adsum, adesse, adfui	be present
adsumo, -ere, adsumpsi, adsumptum	assume
adulter, adulteri, m.	adulterer
adulterium, adulterii, n.	adultery

* advenio, advenire, adveni, adventum	arrive
adventus, -us, m.	arrival, coming
* adversus (prep. + acc., or as adv.)	towards, against
adversus, -a, -um	facing, opposing
advoco, advocare, advocavi, advocatum	summon
aedes *or* aedis, aedis, f.	temple; (pl.) house
aedificatio, -onis, f.	building
aeger, aegra, aegrum	sick
aequalis, -e	equal
Aequi, -orum, m.pl.	the Aequi (an Italian tribe)
aequo, aequare, aequavi, aequatum	equal, match
aetas, aetatis, f.	age, generation, time
* ago, agere, egi, actum	do, act, drive
aio	say
alienus, -a, -um	other, strange
alienus, -i, m.	stranger
* alii . . . alii	some . . . others
alio	in another direction
* aliquis, aliquid	someone, something
* alius, alia, alium	other, different, another
ambages, -ium, f.pl.	riddle
* amicus, -i, m.	friend
* amitto, amittere, amisi, amissum	lose
* amor, amoris, m.	love
amplitudo, -inis, f.	grandeur
amplius	more (than)
* ancilla, -ae, f.	slave-girl
anguis, -is, m.	snake
* animus, animi, m.	spirit, soul mind
* annus, anni, m.	year
* ante (prep. + acc., or as adv.)	before
anteeo, anteire, anteii, anteitum	go before, take the lead
anxius, -a, -um	anxious
Apollo, Apollinis, m.	Apollo
* apud	among; at the house of
Ardea, -ae, f.	Ardea
ardeo, ardere, arsi, arsum	burn

ardor, -oris, m.	eagerness
* argentum, -i, n.	silver
* arma, armorum, n.pl.	arms, weapons
armati, armatorum, m.pl.	armed men
armo, armare, armavi, armatum	arm
Arruns, Arruntis, m.	Arruns
* ars, artis, f.	art, skill
atrox, atrocis	fierce, revolting, horrible
auctor, auctoris, m.	instigator, proposer, doer
* audeo, audere, ausus sum	dare
* audio, audire, audivi, auditum	hear
* aufero, auferre, abstuli, ablatum	take away, remove, steal
aureus, -a, -um	golden, made of gold
* aut	or
* auxilium, auxilii, n.	help
averto, avertere, averti, aversum	turn away, divert
avolo, avolare, avolavi, avolatum	fly away
avunculus, -i, m.	uncle
baculum, baculi, n.	staff
bellator, bellatoris, m.	warrior
* bellum, belli, n.	war
benigne	kindly
* bona, -orum, n.pl.	goods
* bonus, -a, -um	good
brevi	soon, in a short time
Brutus, Bruti, m.	Brutus
* cado, cadere, cecidi, casum	fall
* caedes, caedis, f.	slaughter, murder, death
Caere, indecl., n.	Caere (a town in Etruria)
* capio, capere, cepi, captum	take, seize, catch, capture
captivus, -a, -um	captured
* caput, capitis, n.	head
caritas, caritatis, f.	affection, love
castigator, castigatoris, m.	castigator, reprover
castitas, castitatis, f.	purity, chastity
* castra, castrorum, n.pl.	camp
castus, -a, -um	chaste, pure
* causa, -ae, f.	cause
cavo, cavare, cavavi, cavatum	hollow

Celeres, -um, m.pl.	the Celeres
* **cena, -ae, f.**	dinner
ceno, cenare, cenavi, cenatum	dine, have dinner
centuriata, centuriatorum, n.pl.	by centuries
* **certamen, certaminis, n.**	contest, struggle, conflict
certatim	enthusiastically, with rivalry
* **ceteri, ceterae, cetera**	the others, the rest
ceterum	but
ceterus, -a, -um	the rest of
* **circa**	around, on both sides, near by
cito, citare, citavi, citatum	hasten; summon
* **civis, civis, m. & f.**	citizen
* **civitas, civitatis, f.**	community, citizenship, state
* **clam**	secretly
claudo, claudere, clausi, clausum	close, shut
cloaca, -ae, f.	sewer
* **coepi, coepisse, coeptum**	began
cognomen, cognominis, n.	name, nickname
* **cogo, cogere, coegi, coactum**	collect; force, compel
Collatia, -ae, f.	Collatia
Collatinus, Collatini, m.	Collatinus
colligo, colligere, collegi, conlectum	gather together, collect
columna, -ae, f.	pillar, column
* **comes, comitis, m. & f.**	companion, comrade
comisatio, -onis, f.	revel, drinking party
comiter	courteously, politely
comitia, comitiorum, n.pl.	assembly
commeatus, -us, m.	furlough
commentarius, commentarii, m.	commentary
committo, -ere, -misi, -missum	entrust
commodum, -i, n.	gain, advantage
communis, -e	common, shared
comprimo, -primere, -pressi, -pressum	crush, put down
conatus, -us, m.	attempt, undertaking
concieo, conciere, concivi, concitum	collect, draw together; provoke
concipio, -cipere, -cepi, -ceptum	conceive, draw up, formulate
concito, -are, concitavi, concitatum	rouse, whip up
conclamo, -are, -avi, -atum	cry out, lament, wail

concupisco, -ere, -ii, -itum	long for, covet
* condo, condere, condidi, conditum	found
* coniunx, coniugis, m. & f.	husband or wife
conqueror, conqueri, conquestus sum	complain bitterly of
conscendo, -ere, -scendi, -scensum	mount
* consilium, consilii, n.	plan, advice, design, counsel
consolor, consolari, consolatus sum	console
* consul, consulis, m.	consul
contemptus, -us, m.	contempt, neglect
contingo, -ere, contigi, contactum	touch closely
convenio, -venire, -veni, -ventum	come together; meet
convivium, convivii, n.	entertainment, banquet
cor, cordis, n.	heart
corneus, -a, -um	of cornel-wood
* corpus, corporis, n.	body
* credo, credere, credidi, creditum	believe, trust; believe in
creo, creare, creavi, creatum	elect, appoint
criminatio, criminationis, f.	incrimination
criminor, -ari, criminatus sum	accuse
* crudelis, -e	cruel
cruor, cruoris, m.	blood, gore
cubiculum, cubiculi, n.	bedroom
* culpa, -ae, f.	fault, error, blame
culter, cultri, m.	knife
* cum (+ abl.)	with
* cum (+ subj.)	when, while, since, although
cum ... tum	not only ... but also, both ... and
cupido, cupidinis, f.	desire, ambition
* cura, -ae, f.	care, concern
curia, curiae, f.	senate-house
* curro, currere, cucurri, cursum	run
* custos, custodis, m. & f.	guard
* de (+ abl.)	from, down from; about, concerning
* debeo, debere, debui, debitum	owe; ought, should
decet	it befits, it becomes, it is right
decus, decoris, n.	honour, distinction, glory
decutio, -ere, decussi, decussum	strike off
dedecus, dedecoris, n.	disgrace, dishonour

dedo, dedere, dedidi, deditum	give up, surrender, devote
deduco, deducere, deduxi, deductum	guide, conduct
defero, deferre, detuli, delatum	carry down
defigo, defigere, defixi, defixum	plunge
degenero, -are, -avi, -atum	degenerate
dehinc	from here
* deinde	then, next
delenio, delenire, delenivi	soothe, mitigate
deliberabundus, -a, -um	deep in thought
delictum, delicti, n.	wrong, sin, crime
Delphi, -orum, m.pl.	Delphi
demergo, -mergere, -mersi, -mersum	send underground
desum, deesse, defui	be wanting, be lacking
* deus, dei, m.	god
* dextera, -ae, f.	right hand
* dico, dicere, dixi, dictum	say, speak, tell
* dies, diei, m.	day
* dies, diei, f.	day, set day, appointed day
* dignus, -a, -um (+ abl.)	worthy (of)
dimicatio, dimicationis, f.	contest, struggle, fight
dito, ditare, ditavi, ditatum	enrich; (pass.) enrich oneself
* diu	for a long time
diversus, -a, -um	differing, opposite
divido, -ere, divisi, divisum	divide, distribute
divisus, -us, m.	distribution, division
* divititiae, -arum, f.pl.	riches
* do, dare, dedi, datum	give, grant
* dolus, -i, m.	trick, fraud, deceit, stratagem
domesticus, -a, -um	domestic, of the household
* domus, domus, f., (loc.) domi	house, home
donec	until
* donum, doni, n.	gift
* dormio, dormire, dormivi, dormitum	sleep
* dubius, -a, -um	doubtful, uncertain
ducenti, -ae, -a	two hundred
* duco, ducere, duxi, ductum	lead
dulcedo, -inis, f.	charm, sweetness
duo, duae, duo	two

* **dux, ducis, m.**	leader, general
* **e, ex (+ abl.)**	from, out of, in accordance with
effero, efferre, extuli, elatum	carry out
effigies, effigiei, f.	image, symbol
Egerius, Egerii, m.	Egerius
* **ego, mei**	I
elabor, elabi, elapsus sum	slip out, escape
emitto, emittere, emisi, emissum	send forth, utter
* **enim**	for
* **eo**	there, to that place
* **eo, ire, i(v)i, itum**	go
* **equus, equi, m.**	horse
* **ergo**	therefore
* **erro, errrare, erravi, erratum**	make a mistake
* **et**	and, also
et . . . et	both . . . and
* **etiam**	even, also
Etrusci, Etruscorum, m.pl.	the Etruscans
Etruscus, -a, -um	Etruscan
* **etsi**	even if
ex composito	by agreement, by prearranged plan
ex industria	deliberately, purposefully
exago, exagere, exegi, exactum	drive out
excipio, excipere, excepi, exceptum	receive, take in, welcome; take up, engage in
* **exemplum, exempli, n.**	example, precedent
* **exercitus, -us, m.**	army
exhaurio, -haurire, -hausi, -haustum	exhaust; drain out, cleanse
expeditio, -onis, f.	expedition
expers, expertis	without a share in
expugno, -are, -avi, -atum	storm, take by assault
exsecror, exsecrari, exsectratus sum	curse
exsequor, -sequi, -secutus sum	pursue, punish
* **exsilium, exsilii, n.**	exile
* **exspecto, -are, -avi, -atum**	wait for
exsul, exsulis, m. & f.	exile
exsulo, exsulare, exsulavi, exsulatum	be an exile
exterreo, -ere, -ui, -itum	terrify

extraho, extrahere, extraxi, extractum	draw out
faber, fabri, m.	workman
* **facilis, facile**	easy
* **facio, facere, feci, factum**	do, make
* **fallo, fallere, fefelli, falsum**	deceive, cheat
fateor, fateri, fassus sum	acknowledge, confess
* **fere**	nearly, almost
* **fero, ferre, tuli, latum**	bear, carry; endure; say
* **ferox, ferocis**	bold, warlike, fierce
* **ferrum, ferri, n.**	iron, weapon, sword
fessus, -a, -um	tired
* **fidelis, -e**	faithful, trusty, trustworthy
* **fides, fidei, f.**	trust, faith, trustworthiness; pledge
* **filia, -ae, f.**	daughter
* **filius, filii, m.**	son
* **fio, fieri, factus sum**	be made, be held; happen
flecto, flectere, flexi, flectum	bend, turn
forma, formae, f.	beauty
forsitan	perhaps
* **forte**	by chance
* **fortuna, -ae, f.**	fortune, fate
* **forum, fori, n.**	forum, marketplace
fossa, -ae, f.	ditch
* **frater, fratris, m.**	brother
fraus, fraudis, f.	deceit
frequentia, -ae, f.	large number
* **fuga, fugae, f.**	flight, escape
fundamentum, -i, n.	foundation
furia, furiae, f.	fury, avenging spirit
Gabii, Gabiorum, m.pl. (loc.) Gabiis	Gabii
Gabini, -orum, m.pl.	men of Gabii
Gabinus, -a, -um	of Gabii
* **gaudium, gaudii, n.**	joy
* **gens, gentis, f.**	tribe, race, people
* **gladius, gladii, m.**	sword
Graecia, -ae, f.	Greece
gratus, -a, -um	pleasing
* **habeo, habere, habui, habitum**	have, hold

* **haud**	not
haudquaquam	by no means
heres, heredis, m. & f.	heir
Hernici, -orum, m.pl.	the Hernici (an Italian tribe)
* **hic, haec, hoc**	this
* **hinc**	from here
* **homo, hominis, m.**	man
* **hora, -ae, f.**	hour
* **hortus, horti, m.**	garden
* **hospes, hospitis, m.**	guest, host; stranger
hospitalis, -e	hospitable, for a guest
hostilis, -e	hostile, of the foe
* **hostis, hostis, m. & f.**	enemy
* **iacio, iacere, ieci, iactum**	throw; lay (foundations)
* **iam**	now, already
* **ibi**	there, then
* **idem, eadem, idem**	same
identidem	repeatedly
ignarus, -a, -um	unaware, ignorant
* **ignis, ignis, m.**	fire
ignotus, -a, -um	unknown
* **ille, illa, illud**	that; he, she, it
imitatio, imitationis, f.	imitation
immineo, -ere	overlook; threaten, impend
imperfectus, -a, -um	unaccomplished
* **imperium, imperii, n.**	power, command, empire
* **impetus, -us, m.**	attack, charge
impius, -a, -um	wicked, ungodly
impleo, implere, implevi, impletum	fill
impudicus, -a, -um	unchaste
impune	with impunity, unpunished
* **in (+ abl.)**	in, on
* **in (+ acc.)**	into, onto, for, against
inambulo, -are, -avi, atum	walk in
incalesco, incalescere, incalui	grow hot
incautus, -a, -um	off one's guard
incedo, incedere, incessi, incessum	go, advance; attack, seize
* **incendo, incendere, incendi, incensum**	set on fire, inflame

incensus, -a, -um	set on fire, burning
incido, incidere, incidi, incasum	happen, arise
* incito, incitare, incitavi, incitatum	incite, stir up, urge on
inclino, inclinare, inclinavi, inclinatum	make to waver
inclitus, -a, -um	famous
includo, includere, inclusi, inclusum	enclose, shut up
* inde	from there, then
indico, indicere, indixi, indictum	proclaim, declare
indignitas, indignitatis, f.	indignity, outrage
indignor, indignari, indignatus sum	be indignant at, resent
indignus, -a, -um	unworthy
induo, induere, indui, indutum	put on
industria, -ae, f.	diligence
iners, inertis	useless
infandus, -a, -um	unspeakable, abominable
infestus, -a, -um	hostile
infimus, -a, -um	lowest, weakest, end of
* ingenium, ingenii, n.	character, ability
* iniuria, -ae, f.	injury, injustice, outrage
iniustus, -a, -um	unjust
* inquam, inquit	say
inscius, -a, -um	unaware, unknowing
insitus, -a, -um	innate
insons, insontis	innocent
instituo, instituere, institui, institutum	install, appoint
* instruo, instruere, instruxi, instructum	draw up, train, fashion
insum -esse, -fui	be in
intendo, -ere, intendi, intentum	stretch, deepen
intentus, -a, -um (+ dat.)	intent on, engrossed with
* inter (+ acc.)	among, between, amid
interdum	sometimes, from time to time
* interficio, -ficere, -feci, -fectum	kill
intericio, -icere, -ieci, -iectum	interpose, pass by
interimo, -imere, -emi, -emptum	destroy
interrogo, -are, -avi, atum	ask
intolerabilis, -e	unbearable

invado, invadere, invasi, invasum	attack
inveho, invehere, invexi, invectum	carry in; (pass.) ride into, over
* invenio, invenire, inveni, inventum	find
invidia, -ae, f.	jealousy, unpopularity
inviso, invisere, invisi, invisum	go to see
invisus, -a, -um	hateful
* invito, invitare, invitavi, invitatum	invite
invoco, invocare, invocavi, invocatum	call upon, invoke
* ipse, ipsa, ipsum	self
* ira, irae, f.	anger
* is, ea, id	he, she it; that
* ita	so, thus, in this way
* itaque	and so, therefore
* iter, itineris, n.	journey, route
* iubeo, iubere, iussi, iussum	order
iugulo, iugulare, iugulavi, iugulatum	cut the throat of
iuniores, -ium, m.pl.	juniors, young men
Iunius, Iunii, m.	Junius
Iuppiter, Iovis, m.	Jupiter
iuro, iurare, iuravi, iuratum	swear
ius, iuris, n.	right, privilege, law, justice
iuvenalis, -e	youthful
* iuvenis, iuvenis, m.	young man
iuventa, -ae, f.	youth
iuventus, -utis, f.	youth
iuxta	equally
L. = Lucius, Lucii, m.	Lucius
* labor, laboris, m.	labour, toil
lacrima, -ae, f.	tear
* laetus, laeta, laetum	happy
lana, -ae, f.	wool
lapicida, -ae, m.	stone-cutter
largior, largiri, largitus sum	bestow lavishly
largitio, largitionis, f.	grant, distribution
lateo, latere, latui	lie hidden, lurk
Latium, Latii, n.	Latium
* laudo, laudare, laudavi, laudatum	praise
* laus, laudis, f.	praise, honour

lectus, -i, m.	bed
* lego, legere, legi, lectum	send, select, choose, enrol
* lentus, -a, -um	slow, tedious
* liber, libera, liberum	free
liberator, liberatoris, m.	liberator, deliverer
* liberi, liberorum, m.pl.	children
* libero, liberare, liberavi, liberatum	free
libido, libidinis, f.	desire, lust
ligneus, -a, -um	wooden, of wood
* locus, loci, m.	place
loca, locorum, n.pl.	parts
longe	far, by far
* longus, -a, -um	long
Lucretia, Lucretiae, f.	Lucretia
Lucretius, Lucretii, m.	Lucretius
luctus, -us, m.	grief, mourning
lucubro, lucubrare, lucubravi	work by lamplight
ludibrium, ludibrii, n.	mockery
ludus, -i, m.	game
luxus, -us, m.	luxury
maestitia, -ae, f.	sorrow, sadness
maestus, -a, -um	sad, sorrowful, grief-stricken
* magis	more
magistratus, -us, m.	magistrate
magnificentia, -ae, f.	splendour
maiestas, maiestatis, f.	majesty
malum, mali, n.	evil, woe, disaster
* malus, -a, -um	bad, evil, wicked
mandatum, -i, n.	order, command
* maneo, manere, mansi, mansum	remain, wait
mano, -are, -avi	drip
* manus, -us, f.	hand; power
* mare, maris, n.	sea
* maritus, -i, m.	husband
* mater, matris, f.	mother
maturo, -are, maturavi, maturatum	hasten, do quickly
maxime	especially, chiefly
medium, medii, n.	middle

memoro, -are, -avi, -atum	call to mind, mention, record, relate
* mens, mentis, f.	mind
mentio, mentionis, f.	mention, subject
* metus, -us, m.	fear
* miles, militis, m.	soldier
mina, -ae, f.	threat
minime	no, not at all
minimus, -a, -um	least, youngest
ministerium, ministerii, n.	office, service
minor, -us	less
minus	less, less than
miraculum, miraculi, n.	marvel, wonder
* miror, mirari, miratus sum	be amazed
mirus, -a, -um	wonderful, marvellous, strange
misceo, miscere, miscui, mixtum	mix, mingle, unite
miserabilis, -e	pitiable, wretched
miseria, -ae, f.	misery
* mitto, mittere, misi, missum	send
* modus, -i, m.	manner, way
* moenia, moenium, n.pl.	walls, fortifications
moribundus, -a, -um	dying
* morior, mori, mortuus sum	die
* mors, mortis, f.	death
mortalis, -e	mortal; (pl.) men
motus, -us, m.	movement, uprising
* moveo, movere, movi, motum	move, agitate, stir, begin
muliebris, -e	of a woman, a woman's, womanly
* mulier, mulieris, f.	woman
* multitudo, multitudinis, f.	population, people, multitude, band
* multus, -a, -um	much, many
munifice	generously
munitio, -onis, f.	fortification
* nam	for
natus, -i, m.	son, child
* -ne	... ? (introduces a question)
* ne (+ subj.)	so that ... not

* ne . . . quidem	not even
* nec, neque	and not
* neco, necare, necavi, necatum	kill
necopinatus, -a, -um	unexpected
nefandus, -a, -um	unspeakable, impious, unnatural
* nego, negare, negavi	refuse, deny, say that . . . not
nequaquam	by no means
nequiquam	in vain, to no purpose
ni = nisi	unless
nihil moror, morari, moratus sum	pay no attention to
* nihil	nothing
* nisi	except
nocturnus, -a, -um	of the night, at night
* nomen, nominis, n.	name
* non	not
nosco, noscere, novi, notum	get to know, be acquainted with
* noster, nostra, nostrum	our
* notus, -a, -um	known, familiar
* novus, nova, novum	new, strange
* nox, noctis, f.	night
noxa, -ae, f.	guilt, blame
nudus, -a, -um	naked
* nullus, -a, -um	no, not any
* nuntio, nuntiare, nuntiavi, nuntiatum	announce
* nuntius, nuntii, m.	messenger, message; (pl.) news
nurus, -us, f.	daughter-in-law
o	oh
obeo, obire, obi(v)i, obitum	meet with, perform
oborior, oboriri, obortus sum	rise, well up
* obsideo, obsidere, obsedi, obesessum	besiege
obsidio, -onis, f.	blockade
obstinatus, -a, -um	resolute, stubborn
obtentus, -us, m.	cover, shelter
obvius fieri	meet, encounter
obvius, -a, -um	in the way
* occasio, occasionis, f.	opportunity
* occupo, -are, -avi, -atum	occupy, make busy

occurro, occurrere, occurri, occursum	meet (+ dat.)
* oculus, -i, m.	eye
* odium, odii, n.	hatred
officio, -ere, -feci, -fectum (+ dat.)	eclipse
* omnis, omnis	all, every
opifex, opificis, m.	workmen
opperior, opperiri, oppertus sum	wait for
opportunus, -a, -um	suitable, opportune
opprimo, -ere, oppressi, oppressum	crush, overwhelm, hold down
* [ops], opis, f.	aid, help, energy; (pl.) wealth, power
summa ope	with all possible care
* opus est	there is need of (+ abl.)
opus, indecl., n.	need
* opus, operis, n.	work, deed, labour
oraculum, -i, n.	oracle
* oratio, orationis, f.	speech
orbitas, orbitatis, f.	bereavement
orbus, -a, -um (+ abl.)	deprived (of)
ordine	in turn, in order
* ordo, ordinis, m.	order, class, rank
* oro, orare, oravi, oratum	pray, beg, plead, ask
osculum, osculi, n.	kiss
* otium, otii, n.	peace, rest, free time, leisure
P. = Publius, Publii, m.	Publius
* palam	openly
papaver, papaveris, m.	poppy
* parens, parentis, m. & f.	parent, father or mother
pariter	equally, alike
* paro, parare, paravi, paratum	prepare
* pars, partis, f.	part
parum	too little, not enough
* parvus, -a, -um	small, little
pateo, patere, patui	be open, be evident
* pater, patris, m.	father
* patior, pati, passus sum	suffer, allow, permit
* pauci, -ae, -a	few, a few
pavidus, -a, -um	alarmed, panicked
pavor, pavoris, m.	fear, panic, terror

* pax, pacis, f.	peace
peccatum, peccati, n.	sin, crime
pecco, peccare, peccavi, peccatum	sin
pectus, pectoris, n.	breast, heart
* pecunia, -ae, f.	money
* pello, -ere, pepuli, pulsum	drive back
penes (+ acc.)	in power of, with
* per (+ acc.)	through, throughout; by, during, among
per ambages	in an enigmatical form
percello, -ere, -culi, -culsum	dismay
pererro, -errare, -erravi, -erratum	wander through
perfero, -ferre, -tuli, -latum	bear, carry, convey
* perficio, perficere, perfeci, perfectum	finish, complete
pergo, pergere, perexi, perectum	proceed, hasten
* periculum, periculi, n.	danger
* permitto, -ere, -misi, -missum	hand over, entrust, permit, allow
perpello, perpellere, perpuli, perpulsum	drive, urge
* pervenio, -venire, -veni, -ventum	arrive (at), reach
pestifer, pestifera, pestiferum	deadly
* peto, petere, petivi, petitum	make for, seek for; ask
* plebs, plebis, f.	plebs, common people
plerumque	for the most part
* pono, ponere, posui, positum	place, pitch, put; lay aside
popularis, -e	of the people
* populus, populi, m.	people, nation, tribe
porro	forwards, onwards
* porta, portae, f.	gate
portentum, -i, n.	portent, omen
* possum, posse, potui	be able
* post (+ acc.)	after
* postquam	after
postremo	finally
* potens, potentis	powerful
poto, potare, potavi, potatum	drink
prae (+ abl.)	before
praecipio, -cipere, -cepi, -ceptum	instruct

praecipuus, -a, -um	special
praeco, praeconis, m.	herald
* praeda, praedae, f.	plunder, spoils
praedor, praedari, praedatus sum	plunder
praefectus, prefecti, m.	prefect
praepolleo, -ere, -ui, -itum	be very powerful, be preeminent
praesens, praesentis	present, in person; of the moment, immediate
* praesidium, praesidii, n.	protection, guard
praesto, -stare, -steti, -stitum (+ dat.)	excel
* praeter (+ acc.)	besides, except, in addition to
pravus, -a, -um	evil, improper
premo, premere, pressi, pressum	press hard
prex, precis, f.	prayer
primo	at first
primores, primorum, m.pl.	leading men
* primus, -a, -um	first
* prior, prioris	previous, former
privatus, -a, -um	private
* pro (+ abl.)	instead of, for, before
* procedo, -ere, processi, processum	advance, succeed
prodigium, prodigii, n.	portent, prodigy
* proelium, proelii, n.	battle
profecto	certainly, necessarily
* proficiscor, proficisci, profectus sum	set out
profugio, -fugere, -fugi, -fugitum	flee, escape
prolabor, prolabi, prolapsus sum	fall forwards
promptus, -a, -um	ready; bold
* prope	near
propinquus, -a, -um	near, neighbouring
prudentia, -ae, f.	knowledge
publice	publicly, at public expense
* publicus, -a, -um	public, common, of the state
pudicitia, -ae, f.	modesty
Pythicus, -a, -um	Pythian
quacumque	wherever
quadraginta	forty

* quaero, quaerere, quaesivi, quaesitum	seek, ask
* qualis, -e	of what kind; of such a kind as
* quam	than, as
quandoquidem	since indeed, seeing that
* quantus, -a, -um	how great, how much
quattuor	four
* -que	and
querella, ae, f.	lamentation
* queror, queri, questus sum	complain
qui, quae, quod (interrog. adj.)	what, any
* qui, quae, quod (rel. pron.)	who, which
* quia	because
quicumque, quaecumque, quodcumque	whoever, whatever
* quidam, quaedam, quoddam	a certain
* quidem	indeed
quin (conj.)	moreover, indeed
quin (adv.)	nay!, why . . . not
quinque	five
quis, quis, quid (indefin.)	anyone, anything
* quis, quis, quid	who?, what?
quisnam, quaenam, quidnam	who?, what?
* quisquam, quicquam	anyone, any
* quisque, quaeque, quidque *or* quodque	each
* quisquis, quisquis, quidquid *or* quicquid	whatever
* quo	there, to that place
* quod	because
* quod si	but if
* quoque	also
rapina, rapinae, f.	robbery, plunder
rebello, rebellare, rebellavi, rebellatum	rebel, renew war
* reddo, reddere, reddidi, redditum	return, give back; answer
* redeo, redire, redi(v)i, reditum	return, go back
* refero, referre, retuli, relatum	bring back, report, relate
* reficio, -ficere, -feci, -fectum	make (of money)

regia, -ae, f.	palace, royal house
regio, -onis, f.	district, area
regius, regia, regium	royal, of a king or prince, regal
regno, regnare, regnavi, regnatum	rule, reign, be king
* regnum, regni, n.	kingdom
* relinquo, relinquere, reliqui, relictum	leave (behind)
reor, reri, ratus sum	think, believe
* res, rei, f.	thing, matter, affair, issue, state
* respondeo, -ere, respondi, responsum	reply, answer
* responsum, -i, n.	answer, reply, response
* rex, regis, m.	king
Roma, Romae, f., (loc.) Romae	Rome
Romani, -orum, m.pl.	the Romans
Romanus, -a, -um	Roman, of Rome
* rursus	again
Rutuli, -orum, m.pl.	the Rutuli
saevio, saevire, saevii, saevitum	vent one's rage, be angry
saevitia, -ae, f.	savagery
salvus, -a, -um	safe, well
sane	certainly, by all means
* sanguis, sanguinis, m.	blood
satin = satisne	
* satis	enough, sufficiently
sceleratus, -a, -um	wicked, of crime
* scelus, sceleris, n.	crime, guilt
scilicet	of course
* scio, scire, scivi, scitum	know; (+ inf.) know how to
sciscitor, sciscitari, sciscitatus sum	inquire, question, ask
scriptor, scriptoris, m.	writer, historian
* se, sui, sibi, se	himself, herself, itself, themselves
* sed	but
sedeo, sedere, sedi, sessum	sit
sensim	gradually
sensus, -us, m.	feeling, perception
* sentio, sentire, sensi, sensum	feel, perceive
sepono, -ponere, -posui, -positum	set aside

* **sequor, sequi, secutus sum**	follow
serus, -a, -um	late
servilis, -e	slave-like
Servius, Servi, m.	Servius
servus, servi, m.	slave
seu = sive	or if
seu ... seu	whether ... or
Sex. = Sextus, Sexti, m.	Sextus
* **si**	if, whether
* **simul**	at the same time
simulatio, -onis, f.	assumed appearance
simulo, simulare, simulavi, simulatum	pretend, feign
simultas, simultatis, f.	feud
* **sine (+ abl.)**	without
singuli, -ae, -a	one each, individual
* **sinister, sinistra, sinistrum**	left
* **sino, sinere, sivi, situm**	allow, permit
* **socius, socii, m.**	ally
solitudo, -inis, f.	desert, wilderness,
* **somnus, somni, m.**	sleep
sopio, sopire, sopivi, sopitum	put to sleep
sordidus, -a, -um	base, filthy
* **soror, sororis, f.**	sister
sors, sortis, f.	lot, inheritance; chance, fate; (pl.) oracle
Sp. = Spurius, Spurii, m.	Spurius
Lucretius, Lucretii, m.	Lucretius
speciosus, -a, -um	having a good appearance, plausible
spectatissimum	the decisive proof
spectatus, -a, -um	tested, proved
* **specto, spectare, spectavi, spectatum**	watch, view
specus, -us, m.	cave
* **spes, spei, f.**	hope
stativus, -a, -um	stationary
* **statuo, statuere, statui, statutum**	fix, determine, decide, arrange
stirps, stirpis, f.	family, breed, offspring
stringo, stringere, strinxi, strictum	draw, unsheathe

studio, studere, studui	be eager, desire anxiously
stultitia, -ae, f.	stupidity
stupeo, stupere, stupui	be amazed, be stunned
stupro, stuprare, stupravi, stupratum	debauch
stuprum, stupri, n.	defilement
* sub (+ acc./abl.)	beneath, under
subicio, subicere, subieci, subiectum	put under, make subject, suggest
subitus, -a, -um	sudden
Suessa, ae, Pometia, ae, f.	Suessa Pometia
* sum, esse, fui	be
* summus, -a, -um	highest, greatest, top
superbia, -ae, f.	pride, arrogance
superbus, -a, -um	arrogant, proud
Superbus, Superbi, m.	Superbus
superior, superius	higher, upper; former, earlier
supplex, -icis, m. & f.	suppliant
supplicium, supplicii, n.	punishment
* suus, sua, suum	his, her, its, their (own)
taceo, tacere, tacui, tacitum	be silent, be quiet
* tacitus, -a, -um	silent
taedet, -ere	be wearied
talentum, -i, n.	talent
* talis, tale	such
* tam	so
* tamen	however
tamquam	as if
* tantum	only
* tantus, -a, -um	so great, such a great
Tarquinia, -ae, f.	Tarquinia
Tarquinius, Tarquinii, m.	Tarquinius
* tego, tegere, texi, tectum	cover; protect
* telum, teli, n.	weapon
temere	without good reason
* tempestas, tempestatis, f.	time, season, period
* templum, -i, n.	temple
tempto, -are, temptavi, temptatum	try, attempt
* tempus. temporis, n.	time
tenebrae, -arum, f.pl.	darkness
* teneo, tenere, tenui, tentum	hold

tero, terere, trivi, tritum	wear, waste, spend (time)
* terra, -ae, f.	earth, land
terribilis, -e	terrible
* terror, terroris, m.	terror, fear; danger
testis, testis, m. & f.	witness
* timeo, timere, timui	fear, be afraid
Titus, -i, m.	Titus
* totus, -a, -um	whole, entire
* trado, tradere, tradidi, traditum	hand over
transeo, -ire, -i(v)i, -itum	cross over
transfero, -ferre, -tuli, -latum	transfer, shift
transfugio, -ere, -fugi, -fugitum	flee over to, desert
trepidus, -a, -um	alarmed
tres, tria, trium	three
tribunus, tribuni, m.	tribune
Tricipitinus, -i, m.	Tricipitinus
Tullia, Tulliae, f.	Tullia
Tullius, Tulli, m.	Tullius
* tum	then
* tumultus, -us, m.	uproar, confusion
* tutus, -a, -um	safe
* tuus, -a, -um	your
* ubi	where?, where, when
* ullus, ulla, ullum	any
* ultimus, ultima, ultimum	last
ultor, ultoris, m.	avenger, revenger
ultro	of one's own accord
* unde	from where
unus, una, unum	one
urbanus, -a, -um	urban, of a city
* urbs, urbis, f.	city
usquam	anywhere
* ut	as, when, how; that, so that, to
* uter, utra, utrum	which of the two
* uterque, utraque, utrumque	both, each (of two)
* uxor, uxoris, f.	wife
Valerius, Valerii, m.	Valerius
vanus, vana, vanum	empty, vain, untrue
vates, vatis, m. & f.	prophet, soothsayer

* -ve	or
vehiculum, vehiculi, n.	chariot, carriage
* velut	as if, as it were
* venio, venire, veni, ventum	come
* verbum, verbi, n.	word
* vero	indeed, really
verso, versare, varsavi, versatum	turn, occupy
* verto, vertere, verti, versum	turn
* verus, -a, -um	true
vestigium, vestigii, n.	footprint, trace
* vestis, vestis, f.	clothing, robe, dress
* veto, vetare, vetui, vetitum	forbid, tell not
* vetus, veteris	of long standing, old, ancient
* via, viae, f.	road, way
viam flectere	make a circuit
* victor, victoris, m.	conqueror, victorious, conquering
victrix, victricis, f.	conqueror, victorious, conquering
* video, videre, vidi, visum	see
* videor, videri, visus sum	seem
viginti	twenty
vigor, vigoris, m.	vigour
* vinco, vincere, vici, victum	defeat, overcome
vinum, vini, n.	wine
violo, violare, violavi, violatum	violate
* vir, viri, m.	man, husband
* vis, vim, vi, f., (pl.) vires	force, violence; (pl.) strength
visus, -us, m.	apparition, sight
* vivo, vivere, vixi, victum	live
* voco, vocare, vocavi, vocatum	call, summon
Volesus, Volesi, m.	Volesus
* volo, velle, volui	want
Volsci, -orum, m.pl.	the Volsci
voluntarius, voluntarii, m.	volunteer
* vos, vestrum	you
* vox, vocis, f.	voice, sound
* vulnus, vulneris, n.	wound

Printed in the USA
CPSIA information can be obtained
at www.ICGtesting.com
LVHW020856171024
794056LV00002B/565

9 781350 060388